Transmissions from Home

Transmissions from Home

Nancy Horn

Balboa Press books may be ordered through booksellers or by contacting:

Balboa Press
A Division of Hay House
1663 Liberty Drive
Bloomington, IN 47403
www.balboapress.com
1-(877) 407-4847

Printed in the United States of America

ISBN: 978-1-4525-4968-2 (sc)
ISBN: 978-1-4525-4967-5 (e)

Balboa Press rev. date: 5/10/2012

This book is dedicated to Mother Earth for sustaining all life on her beautiful blue planet. To all those from the Galactic Federation of Light who came forth with these loving messages and who continue to walk with me on my journey. Without you, this book would not be. Also, to all those who have come into my "earthly existence" as family, friends and teachers. Each and every one has a special place in my heart. Always, with love and light.

Dear reader:

At the beginning of 2007, I began to receive messages from the Galactic Federation of Light. These messages were always given in a loving nature. As you read through the book, you will see they wanted to have personal contact with us years ago but circumstances here on earth were not favorable.

The word "soon" was often used in these messages. In our earthly 3D realm, we operate within "linear" time. The Galactics operate in "no time", so their sense of the word "soon" is not the same as ours. It's as different as a day is to a year.

These transmissions are my truth. By having them put into print for all to read, I hope one will come away with the sense of having "met a few new friends". These are certainly exciting times we are living in. Mother Earth and humanity are going through a huge shift in consciousness. The Galactics have taught me not to be afraid of change. Our change will be all and more than what we've ever hoped for. And our friends will be with us every step of the way.

In love and light
Nancy Horn
2012

YEAR 2007

Sunday, March 11, 2007

We are here to assist you. You have sensed us since the beginning of 2007. What is it you desire? Speak to us. You feel us within the very fiber of your being; the coldness; for we are trying to get your attention. Speak to us; we desire dialogue between you and those that surround you. Yes, we ARE here to assist. Do not feel as though you have to walk your path alone. You are surrounded by many who love you more than you could imagine. We know that you feel our love and we also feel yours. Ask your questions; you will receive your answers. We will answer you through your great love of music. Oh yes, we know your soul hungers for music, it always has. We play songs for you that have a special meaning for you. Do you hear songs played time and again that you love? That is us, letting you know we are here. Great things are going to be happening soon in rapid succession and we need your attention at all times. The world needs you; listen to us for guidance. We are in service to you as you are in service to humanity. You are a gift to this world; let us help. We honor you always as a fellow light being.

Tuesday, March 13, 2007

We are here. Talk to us. What is it you wish to know? We communicate by thought process. Never push away your thoughts for we are talking to you. Did we not just play another song for you? Listen to the words of this song, "I Hope You Dance". This is what we wish for you; to grab hold of your dreams and run with them. You have so much to offer others; don't hide behind a mask of self-doubt. That is not you. You are wise beyond the lines of this dimension. Do you not visit us here in the light cities in the sky while you are at work? Time and space mean nothing to those who time travel; you have been doing this for a long time. This is not something new to you. Come to us for guidance, we are always around. You have asked us about teaching people of love. We certainly approve and will have further communication on this topic. We also know there are many activities you wish to participate in; just pace yourself. Too much at once will deplete your energy. Further communication on this topic will also follow. For now, just ride the winds of change and know in your heart you are forever loved and admired by your fellow light beings.

Saturday, March 17, 2007

Go ahead, we are here. We know it's very frustrating for you at the best of times; please be strong and hold on for awhile longer. It is not yet the right time for your answers. Please be patient; what you are asking for is coming to fruition. You feel it in your heart; the desire. But first it has to manifest in all ways. This is a two-sided equation. You are very much alike. Neither likes significant change but it will be for the greatest good of both and for the greatest good of all. That is all we can say, please, just be patient and we promise it will be worth the wait. We love and honor you always.

Wednesday, March 21, 2007

Yes, we are here. We honour you this day, a day of truths. That which you desire is coming to fruition. You have asked about teaching of eternal love; wait patiently, all the players are not yet in place. In the meantime, yes, search for your stones. You will find them; they are awaiting you. Whenever you are feeling yourself falling within the depths of despair, think of us. We are forever around you. Take a deep breath and feel our love surrounding you like a warm cloak. YOU ARE NEVER ALONE.

Ashtar sends his love and echoes your sentiments "Nancy Rocks"! Peace to you on this grand day. You are forever honored as a fellow light being.

Sunday, March 25, 2007

Good evening, Nancy! Greetings to you and yours. We know this time of waiting and manifestation is very nerve wracking for you at the best of times. Please be patient; timing is everything. We know you feel change is coming. Walking toward the unknown is always challenging. Life itself is never an open book. There may be twists and turns and even periods of complete solitude. Take this period of your life now for quiet contemplation. We have been giving you many sacred signs and are very pleased at your progress. Don't forget to pay attention to signs that are repeated time and again. These are very important and speak to your heart. As you know, we have been giving you many "Lakota" signs since the fall of 2006. We are pleased to see you are following through with research into the Sioux people. This is extremely important. Please don't let up on your studies. Remember, knowledge is power. Whenever you need our assistance, we are only a thought away. We cherish you, dear one, for you are loved beyond this dimension.

Friday, March 30, 2007

Greetings Nancy! You have had quite a surprise today. We have told you this day was coming, a day of miracles, the reason for your "Lakota" signs. Your return has been prophesized by the Sioux people for a long time now. Wonderful new and exciting changes will be happening in the next while but for now just get used to the idea of who you really are. There will be tremendous responsibility but we know you are quite capable of handling it. There will be times when you are in danger; always be aware of your surroundings and remember we will be around to protect you. As we have told you before, just ride the winds of change and cherish every moment. You are loved, dear one, more than you know.

Wednesday, April 4, 2007

Yes, go ahead; we are here. Have faith, you ARE hearing these messages. We have heard your request for a vision; it will come. Please just take some quiet time for yourself. Your life is going to change quite dramatically. We know it is hard to envision just what is going to come about. We informed you last year there would be huge energy changes this year, not just for you, but the world in general. This year of enlightenment will be a huge eye opener for many. It is time for the vibrations of light and love to infuse the world with their strong messages. You, dear one, are one of those messages. Go forth in faith. We stand beside you.

Saturday, April 7, 2007

Greetings Nancy! It is time for another milestone in your life; the time to tell others of your return. These people will present themselves to you; you may know of them already. Do not fear what will come to be; we are here to assist you in your journey. This is a time of great wonderment for you and for all. Hold your head high and always walk in spirit, for people will want your guidance. Lead with your heart; it will never betray you. An abundance of blessings to you, dear one, on your most sacred journey of all.

Sunday, April 15, 2007

Greetings, dear one! We sense your confusion. This confusion can only leave if you let it; this is done by telling others. Yes, you know who you must tell; we have made it very obvious to you. Please don't be frightened, dear one. It truly is fear of the unknown, not fear of your sacred path. Nothing is given to you that you cannot handle. We will assist you. The more you learn to walk in peace, the more your path ahead is illuminated. Shine your light, dear one, and be a welcome beacon to the world.

Sunday, April 22, 2007

Greetings, dear one! What a wonderful time for you and for others that surround you! A wondrous time for magical manifestation. Just keep thinking positive thoughts and all will be well. Enormous changes are at hand. This sense of urgency you feel will only get stronger till all has come to be. The heavens sing your praises, dear one, and surround you at this very unique time in your life. You ask if there are any blockages that must be surrendered before the manifestation process is complete. No, dear one, for you it is clear sailing ahead. Everything will be taken care of; there is not to be worried about. All is well and unfolding as is expected. Just remember, timing is everything. Be joyous, shine your light and love like never before. That is all we ask at this time. Surrender everything else to us. Enjoy walking your sacred path and allow others to walk in your footsteps. Blessings from all in love and light.

Sunday, April 29, 2007

Greetings, dear one! Bravo to you! We know this contact has been hard for you and it did not transpire as you had hoped. Please be patient; all is well. The process is now well on its way; it will only lead to great things. You spoke tonight from your heart; that is all that matters. The rest will transform and manifest into reality. Great things always take time. Look beyond the obvious to see the truth. The truth, as it is, will not be easy for some to accept. Let us refer back to the reason for this contact. When you were told your truth, was it not hard for you to grasp and accept? Now is the time for patience as others learn the truth they have to accept. The energy is now accelerating at a faster pace and ALL eventually will be faced with the truth. This is to be and is not for the faint of heart. Stand your ground, be positive and everyone will come to see your truth. You know who you are. Walk with ease and grace; you are forever loved. Be at peace. Blessings of love and light to you on this day of truths.

Saturday, May 19, 2007

Greetings Nancy! It has been awhile since our last communication. Stay focused and we assure you great things will be happening. The stars have awaited this reunion for many eons. Dreams DO manifest into reality; it just takes time. The universe awaits with baited breath for this moment. All is according to plan and cannot be altered. We love you, dear one. All sing your praises for this most difficult journey. You will never walk alone. Go in peace.

Tuesday, May 29, 2007

NANCY: *I think I deserve some hard answers to questions I have been asking and I will ask again. Why all the "Lakota" signs?*
ANSWER: Because you are White Buffalo Calf Woman. We had to introduce you to the Lakota heritage before telling you who you really are. We will keep giving you these signs till you have fully accepted it. We understand that it's hard to grasp.
NANCY: *You have told me to "tell others" of my existence. Yet, when I do, I just receive their "spin" on the information I'm giving them. Or else, maybe they're not receiving the right information from spirit. If so, why do I feel as though I'm wasting my breath trying to tell others when they are not grasping the situation?*
ANSWER: We have told you before, all are not privy to the same information. The reason we wanted you to tell of your existence is to start the thought process in others minds. And don't think for one minute people aren't thinking of the possibility! If you didn't tell someone of your existence, how could we get the ball rolling, so to speak? We feel your frustration and want you to know this shall pass and everyone will soon see the light. We did explain to you at the beginning of the year that this would be a year of learning for you. Have you not had a major breakthrough already? Please, just take your time ingesting this information. It is of the utmost importance that you fully accept who you really are. Take your time; there is no rush on this. It is what it is. You do not need to "ask"

others who you are when you already know the answer to the question. It's in your heart.

NANCY: *Dan and I have, I think, really put ourselves out there this last weekend, driving down and back to South Dakota in four days. As you know, we are not very financially stable like a lot of other people. We really couldn't afford this trip but went anyway. I was also led to believe there was an "urgent reason" for going down. Please explain because I'm not comprehending the reason behind any of this.*

ANSWER: Let us begin at the beginning. As far as your financial situation, yes, we know how bad off you think you are; but really, aren't all your needs being met? You have a roof over your head, food to eat and yes, your bills are getting paid. Right now you have to work hard to keep yourselves above water. Remember, this is a year of learning and not all lessons are easy. You have it easier than many other people in this world. Abundance will come when abundance is needed and not before. The reason for this trip, and yes you were pushed to go, was another learning experience for you. How can you work with people you know absolutely nothing about? You could see for yourself how these people live on their reserves; not a pretty picture was it? Yet, they still hold their heads high and live life to the fullest, with a smile on their face and a wave of their hand in greeting to complete strangers. Get the picture yet? You cannot work with people if you do not assimilate the same values yourself. Another lesson learned. As far as meeting a certain person, it did not happen last weekend. Does that mean never to you? Does that mean you should give up? Or does that mean you should push forward with a smile on your face, a wave of your hand to complete strangers you meet. Nancy, this world is full of "hard truths" to your "hard answers". YOU HAVE TO LEARN TO FIND THE DEEPER MEANING YOURSELF. We are not mad or angry at you. You are a child of light and very much loved; more than you know. We truly understand the hardships but want you to know they are there for a reason. Learn and grow, that is what this year is all about, nothing else.

Wednesday, June 6, 2007

NANCY: *Dan and I are planning a trip back to South Dakota. Are we being directed to do this or is this something we think needs to be done?*
ANSWER: Yes, you ARE being directed to take this trip. As we have told you before, this is a year of learning. You are being directed to places with historical significance. Knowledge is power. You can't go into the next few years totally blinded to what and who you are dealing with. There will be many hardships ahead, all in the name of learning.
NANCY: *What exactly do you mean by hardships?*
ANSWER: Hardships, as in everything isn't always going to go perfectly as you have seen in your last trip. I don't mean complete disasters; just know not everything will always be perfect or you wouldn't learn.
NANCY: *You have used the term* "I" *in your last statement. Who are you?*
ANSWER: My name is Ashtar. Hello Nancy! It has been awhile since our last communiqué. Thank you for not answering the phone; it would have broken our transmission. I'm quite worried about your eating patterns lately; no meat, some meat, no junk food, lately lots of junk food. Please, please, please, correct yourself in this matter. Lots of fruits and vegetables, grains, rice, a lot of what you were eating was o.k. Please, absolutely no fattening snacks and no meat. Your weight is back down to where it was before your last trip. Lets try and get it further down over the summer months. It is imperative that you lose the weight this year as the next few years will be very active years for you. Tell Daniel I'm counting on him to help you along as he travels the same road himself. Daniel, please cut back on your pop consumption. It is all right to have the odd "snack night"; everything in moderation. I am extremely proud of the progress that both of you are making. It takes great strides to come where you were a year ago to the two people I know now. Not everyone would have been able to go through what both of you have and still be able to function in their everyday lives. Nancy, we know you have been going through some turmoil's lately; stay strong, be brave, and all will be well.
NANCY: *As you know, my friend passed away last weekend. Is she O.K.?*

ASHTAR: Yes, she is fine. She came through the veil and is reunited with her family. It takes awhile to adjust to being home again, so she is receiving a lot of loving care right now. Do not worry about her; she is fine.
NANCY: *I haven't been feeling well lately. Is there something wrong with me?*
ASHTAR: No, nothing that a proper diet and some rest won't cure. As I have stated before, stay on a healthy diet, keep exercising and please get plenty of rest. You have just gone through a stressful time that has taken its toll on your body. Remember, it is the vehicle in which you live. Take care of it.
NANCY: *Ashtar, is there anything else you wish us to know at this time?*
ASHTAR: No, we will be communicating now and again. Listen to your guides; they care so much about you. Daniel, my friend. I want you to know you can be doing this also. In fact, try it tonight. There are those who want to communicate with you also. Go in love and light. I'm always around if you need me; just call.

Thursday, June 7, 2007

Nancy: *In the next few years, I know part of my job will be teaching others. As White Buffalo Calf Woman, what could I be teaching the natives that they don't already know? I know nothing of the teachings of White Buffalo Calf Woman; are we the same spirit.........different spirits?? Me knowing nothing of before?? This is confusing to me.*
Answer: We will answer the latter part of your question first. You carry the "essence" or spirit of the previous White Buffalo Calf Woman. In earlier times, she came to the Sioux people and taught them their sacred ceremonies. She told them of her return; that is where you come in. She came to them long ago in human form as you are doing also. Two different "human vehicles", same essence. You do not need to remember what came about before; it is not pertinent to today's teachings. Yes, you will be teaching the Sioux as well as many others. The teachings will involve peace, love and harmony among mankind. You will become a bridge so to speak. This is all we will say for now on this topic; more will come later.

Remember, taking on too much at once will deplete your energy. One thing at a time. Surround yourself with historical knowledge for now. Don't get too caught up in all the little details. Have fun with this and keep a smile on your face. All is well.

Nancy: *When Dan and I are out and about shopping and bump into native people, quite often we find them staring at us. Yet, when we were down in South Dakota, the same scenario didn't seem to take place. Why is this? Just curious.*

Answer: You have to remember there are only a hundred thousand light bearers on earth so to speak. That is spread over the whole planet!! Not a lot, compared to the population of the planet is it? That is the reason for the stares….the light and the loving energy coming from you. Both of you are a rare commodity. As for South Dakota, the Sioux are very spiritual people. Nancy, as you have read, the Sioux do not "stare" when around their elders. They keep their eyes lowered out of respect. Another lesson learned. Of course they noticed both of you, more than you realize. They just didn't make it obvious by staring; out of respect to both of you. Two completely different cultures.

Nancy: *Thank you for answering my question.*

Answer: You are most welcome. Peace and love to you, dear one.

Monday, June 11, 2007

Greetings Nancy! You seem to be very scattered lately. Please correct this as it isn't doing you or us any good. You seem to be worried about a lot of little things that don't make sense to us. Let it all go and concentrate on what makes your heart happy. Also, please try to meditate on a more regular basis as this is how your guides communicate with you. You must be constantly communicating with them also. They are your earthly helpers. Big changes are coming soon. Be prepared. Take care of yourself and you will soar with the eagles. All is well; go in peace. You are forever loved.

Monday, June 18, 2007

NANCY: *I've been told there are a few things I should be concentrating on right now. Should I keep on with the language? What should I be learning now?*
ANSWER: Greetings Nancy! Right now focus on maintaining your light; make sure you are projecting it out to others. Yes, by all means familiarize yourself with the language. As we have explained before, you are already fluent in this language. It is locked away in your cellular memory and will be unleashed when the time is right.
NANCY: *What is it exactly that I will be doing?*
ANSWER: You will be teaching others how to live in peace and harmony. Also, what it is like where you come from.

Thursday, June 28, 2007

NANCY: *Hello friends! I'm sorry I'm coming to you in such a state. You know about the contents of the email I received this morning. I'm just trying to keep myself healthy and sane at this point. Any pointers would help at this time.*
ANSWER: Greetings Nancy! Yes we did read the email; in fact, we sent it. We've informed you not all lessons will be easy. You can only do what you can do. Everyone else has their own life to deal with and you have yours. Don't let them run you down. We know it's very difficult. Are you going to let this scenario stop you from your life? This is up to you. Yes, we can advise you but we can't make your decisions for you. Just listen to your heart. We love you, dear one.

Friday, July 6, 2007

Greetings Nancy! We come to you today to tell you what is coming next. In the days to come, you will be feeling our presence much more than you have ever before. It is time for us to start working as a team. You have seen fleeting glimpses of white lately in your peripheral vision; that is us. We are around you all the time. You will start to feel an acceleration of energy; everything is being bumped up ahead of schedule. Such exciting times! This is what you have come down here for…your grand purpose. Shine on, baby! You are through some of the tough stuff now and for awhile it is smooth sailing ahead. We are sorry about your trip but there were still lessons for you to learn. For now, we want you to grab hold of this dream of yours and run; even soar with it. You know who you are; a great prophecy coming to life! Won't people be stunned! Certain people think they have you pegged as one thing, when really you are someone else. White Buffalo Calf Woman comes to life! And they think she comes when white buffalo calves are being born! Oh no….that's not it at all. You've already been here since 1956, living right under everyone's noses! We anticipate the looks on the faces when the truth finally reveals itself. As we have told you before, these times are not for the faint of heart. There is going to be great upheaval when everyone learns what's really going on. Please, keep talking to us in the days ahead. For now, this is how we are communicating. Rest up, dear one, and take care of yourself. You are forever loved and admired by your fellow peers. Take care.

Sunday, July 8, 2007

Greetings Nancy! This communiqué will be short as not much has changed since the last one. Thank you for brilliantly showing your light yesterday as there were many who saw it. Not all understood but there were few who knew you would soon be someone of great stature. Those few were very thankful to the creator for having you bless their powwow with your presence. Once again, thank you dear one, for following your heart. Blessings of love and light to you.

Saturday, July 14, 2007

Greetings Nancy! It has been awhile since our last communiqué'. Everything is falling according to plan. Enjoy your time with your family.

Your presence there is calming the situation entirely. We know it is hard for you to be separated from your own home but as time goes on, this will be a reality for you. Keep your feet firmly planted on the ground and know in your heart all is well. Blessings to you and yours.

Sunday, July 15, 2007

Greetings Nancy! The time is very much at hand. We are so glad to hear of your excitement. It won't be long now. There is a lot of high energy spinning the air. This is the reason you feel disconnected from everyone and everything. It is what it is. Enjoy!

Saturday, July 21, 2007

Greetings, dear one! This communiqué is about following your heart. We know your heart is full of love for everyone and that times are frustrating. Just remember, not everyone is the same. What one person sees as love, another sees disaster; something to run from. There are those you find hard to be around as there are those that find it hard to be around you. Too mush light spells disaster for some people. At this time, learn the differences in people's own frequencies. There are many who will be frightful of you; show them much love and all will be well. Shine your light and live from the heart.

Sunday, July 22, 2007

Greetings, dear one! Thank you for stating your heart's desire. That's all you have to do and it is so. The one's that you miss, miss you also. And it is so.

Thursday, July 26, 2007

Greetings Nancy! The hard times are just about over. Try to get through these next days with ease and grace. The glorious sun is peeking over the horizon and all is beautiful. Have fun with your new job as it will be much more than your wildest dreams. That is it for now; keep charging ahead. Much love to you and yours from your friends.

Tuesday, July 31, 2007

Greetings Nancy! We have been waiting to connect with you once again. Yes, we know you are tired of your job. It will soon be over and you will be on to bigger and better things. This is taking some time but will be worth it in the end. You are wondering how all of this will come about. The key lies in remembering who you are. Once that has occurred, everything else will fall into place. Then people will be forced to look and see who you are. No worries; everything will work out. Yes, this will start this year; everything has been bumped ahead. Just stay on course; everything is as it should be for now. Much love to you on your incredible journey.

Sunday, August 5, 2007

Greetings Nancy! Such wonderment at the powwow! Everything that you thought was going on, WAS going on! It was not your imagination. More and more people are getting curious and that's exactly what we want to see. The more you put yourself out there, the more known you will become. You are going to be the talk of Wikwemikong for weeks to come. They know you are some sort of holy person and you were there to bless the festivities with your presence. Job well done! You also, Dan! Much love to you both. You're forever in our hearts.

Wednesday, August 8, 2007

Greetings Nancy! It has been a day of wondrous miracles, has it not? Lots of Dakota trucks, not having to work very hard today and you have finally made a new friend. Oh yes, both you and Dan will get to know him very well over the next few months. What better way is there to get to know the natives than to actually get to know one. Yes, we will also tell Dan. At this time we just wanted you to know that his arrival was planned in the stars. Please don't waste this opportunity. Blessings on this relationship and to you all.

Friday, August 10, 2007

Greetings Nancy! The time has certainly come. Do not fear what is to come. You are as ready now as you'll ever be. Sometimes learning and doing are one and the same. The heavens are behind you one hundred percent. Enjoy the ride child, you deserve it. Honor us well. Follow your heart; it will always lead you home. The stars are watching; go get'em girl! Shine your light, our little angel. Blessings to you. Your world is our oyster.

Sunday, August 12, 2007

Greetings Nancy! Please do not give up on us. You are needed. You have to believe you have an important job to do here on earth. Everything IS going according to plan. We have told you that things are starting to happen. NOW BELIEVE IT! You are going to see evidence of this. We hear your questions and we will answer to the best of our ability so you can understand. Yes, we are truly aware of your financial situation. The only thing we can say is it takes time to manifest it from here to there. So many factors have to be bang on to work together - energy shifting, portal openings and keeping a positive faith that all is well. Meditation helps us a lot; we know you are pinched for time but we need both you and Dan more here with us through meditation. Nancy, there are those at your work who are privy to what is going on with you and Dan and are working against anything positive happening for the two of you. You may know who they are. Nancy, you are now in a situation where you are not in one spot all day. It is impossible for you to connect spiritually with us. This is one example of what has taken place. This is why, when both you and Dan are at home, we need to have more of your undivided attention to counteract what is going on at work. We ARE going to prevail but it will take more work than what was previously believed. You see, where you are, free will is the dominant playing factor and we have to work around it. No Nancy, when we mean "privy to what is going on" we are talking that they know there is something special with the two of you and people are trying to disseminate it. Just remember, both of you, to shoot "pink" at these people and lots of it! They do not know who you will become; that is being kept secret just as our communiqués are secret. Both you and Dan are highly protected. No one can read your thoughts; that was agreed upon before you both came down to earth. We are truly sorry for all that is happening but because of free will it is making our job that much more complicated. But as we have said before, WE WILL PREVAIL because too many galaxies are watching and waiting for this thing not to happen. It is just taking time. Please, please, please, more meditation at home. Somehow, please see that this happens. We need this assignment to start soon and we are doing are part at this end. Yes Nancy, what you are thinking about at this time is exactly what is going on. But he is very confused right now; a person is putting thoughts into his head. He knows he was sent to your work for a reason (maybe you?) but he is being influenced by the wrong people. Don't worry, this matter is going to be rectified shortly. We have a back-up plan in motion now as we speak. We want to point out to you how well your intuitive side is working. Whenever you feel uncomfortable in someone's presence, send them light then back away. That is it for now; please again, more meditating and anytime you have more questions, just talk to us. We are always around. Much love to you both.

Wednesday August 15, 2007

Greetings Nancy! We know these times are tough for you. You are being prepared for big changes. The times are near. Thank you for meditating more; it is helping our cause greatly. We will have further communication later. Remember, all is well. You are loved.

Saturday, August 18, 2007

Greetings Nancy! Manifestation has begun. Your world for the next few weeks will be very topsy-turvy. There will be many changes at hand; all good. Look upon these as wondrous new times. Your heart and soul will soar as never before. It will seem as everything has finally come together; all mysteries are solved and it all makes sense. Your real work will not start till next year as the rest of this year is for your own benefit. With only five years left, you will assume your role. All is well; take one day at a time and run with it. Be joyous, happy and carefree, dear one. You are most loved.

Monday, August 20, 2007 (called in Ashtar)

Yes Nancy, I am here. You are worrying far too much. You have been told not to worry at all. Relax, everything is fine. You have been questioning your meditations. Don't. Everything you hear is really being said to you. You MUST TRUST this! This is all part of the great plan. Have fun, be full of wonderment. The cycle is progressing faster and faster and you will very soon see proof of this. Yes, you and Dan will have some time for yourselves to do some traveling. The Archangel Michael would like you both to go to Lake Louise on your way to B.C. Nancy, you know the energy is shifting higher now; you feel it. It is very much like feeling light-headed. Almost like you're feeling "high", which is exactly what is happening. This will only expand further which gets us back to the reason you will not be able to work soon. As this "high" feeling becomes greater, it will be dangerous for you both to be working around machinery. Always keep this thought in your mind for you know it to be true. I am extremely proud of the progress the two of you have made. There is much excitement here over what the two of you have shown us. We are so proud! Keep forging ahead - not long now and the REAL living starts! I love you both.

Thursday, August 23, 2007 (Ashtar)

Greetings Nancy! Thank you for talking with me. I know you're very disappointed right now. The money is there but you have to keep a positive attitude. You will head to Lake Louise soon; it is imperative you go there. This is where your "coming out" takes place, so to speak. Enjoy your last few days in your "old life" as your new life will be very hectic to say the least. Think positive and always with love. Blessings to you both.

Saturday, September 1, 2007 (Ashtar)

Yes Nancy, I am here. Thank you for speaking with me. I want to tell you that of lately all of the thoughts that are forming in your mind are divinely guided. All of your hopes and aspirations are coming to fruition. Please believe this. Keep watching for signs as these are also guiding you. This year is swiftly closing to an end. There is much to be done yet but I know both you and Dan are up to the challenge and will be quite successful. Keep thinking positive thoughts for the years to come as they are going to be some of the best this world has ever seen. You can take that statement to the bank along some greenery you might want to take there also. Thank you for writing that down. I know it's a sore subject with you right now. Your guides are missing you tremendously; please go and visit them more often as they are working with you also to bring about a positive outcome. Nancy, you know who you are and MUST work with these native guides. They so wanted to come in and work with you; please don't let them down. You know your story and have worked with the natives before. What a blessing and opportunity to be given that chance again! Blessings to you and Dan and keep up the good work, my friends.

Monday, September 3, 2007 (Ashtar)

Yes Nancy, I am here. Go ahead. Your awakening will come in stages. If it were to happen all at once, it would be too much of a shock to handle. The awakening will be in knowledge of subjects that you had no prior knowledge of. This burst of knowledge will increase until you become the person you are destined to be. This will also happen to Dan but you both won't be knowledgeable in the same areas. Therefore, together you will be most valuable. Remember to get plenty of rest as this will still be a shock to your systems. You will basically still be the same people, just more knowledge, much more confidence and you will be able to speak in large crowds. Don't worry, all is well. Be good to yourselves and others. Shine your light and always send love to others. Blessings to you both.

Sunday, September 9,2007

Greetings Nancy! Lovely magical day yesterday at the powwow. Lots of spirit; lots of dancing makes for good times. You are getting stronger and stronger; don't stop. Keep it happening. As you can see, it's important to go to these events as you are putting yourself out there for all to see. And boy, can they see! You give them what they want; spirit.! Everyone here gives you their love. Keep shining; give love to all!

Wednesday, September 12, 2007

Greetings Nancy! All is well. Magical manifestations happening behind the scenes. Keep shining on! You are making quite a name for yourself around the area! Just as we expected! Wonderful, wonderful. Energy accelerating now. The candle has been lit and the flame is burning high, so to speak. Both you and Dan brought so much love and hope to the powwow last weekend. These people can't thank you both enough. A lot of spirit felt by all. It was quite a celebration for them. Do you see now? This is what you do for others. Gives them hope for a brighter tomorrow. Congratulations to both of you. Job well done. Blessings to you both. We love you dearly.

Friday, September 14, 2007

Greetings Nancy, to you on this fine day. Keep up the wonderful work, all is well. We here, on Starship 3, miss you very much. Everything going according to plan. The council is very pleased on how everything is progressing. It won't be long now till the real work begins. Prepare yourself. Your sleep patterns are very irregular because of all the data being stored in your subconscious. We are truly amazed that you can function at all. You told us, eons ago, you were capable of this and you were right. You are truly a wonder to us all. We send you our love, compassion and always hold you in a place of honor.

Sunday, September 16, 2007

Good afternoon Nancy! Greatness manifesting. Good things to all. It will happen more quickly than you think. As transcribed earlier, we are pleased with the progress being made as to the reason for your earthly visit. The gates will be opened soon and the butterfly shall fly free. You then shall make many changes and your planning shall begin. Look forward to working with people we are presenting to you. They will come swiftly and you will know who they are. Always remember this is a job but we also want you to have fun with it. All is well; keep shining your light. Call to us in your dreams; we will talk to you and present ourselves. Please light more candles within your home; it is a signal to us. This too is our way of communicating. Listen to your thoughts; we will never lead you astray. Your emerging will come swiftly. This will not be a frightful time for you as these things and thoughts emerge. This is just a time of remembering for you; a "how did I ever forget this" type of feeling. A remembering of who you really are. That is all. When this happens, you will also remember your mission. Many blessings to you and Dan and to the many you will work with. We expect this to be a total success. Much love and light.

Wednesday, September 19, 2007

Greetings Nancy! The time has come; be prepared. Many things happening at once. It will be like a sudden impact of goodness. All things blessed. Have a great time with this. Remember, you will never be alone. Your welfare is always looked after. Go with ease and grace. Blessings to those that surround you at this time. Go forward with peace in your heart. You are forever loved.

Saturday, September 22, 2007

Greetings Nancy! It is a wonderful day, is it not? Many greetings and blessings to Dan this day; the day of his birth. We wish to tell you of the success of this project. It has been an amazing ride, has it not? Everything manifesting rapidly now. Are you both ready? The time is drawing near. To us, back home, this project has already surpassed our wildest dreams. Bravo to both of you. Keep it going; the wonderful love and energy emerging from the two of you. Nancy, we wish to tell you the thoughts you have had today are very close to the way things will take form. With, of course, a few twists and turns to make it much more interesting. Blessings to the two of you and start looking to a glorious future. All is well; keep the faith.

Tuesday, September 25, 2007

Greetings dear one! This day has been filled with peace and contentment but also a little disappointment. People come in and out of your life for a reason, although you may not know the reason at the time. Just remember, everything and every situation is a learning experience. We know the disappointment stems from not becoming better friends but who knows what the future might hold. Acknowledge your feelings and let them go for you have other matters you must concentrate on at the moment. We know you have dreams of going out west before the snow flies. Keep the faith; we hear your pleas. All is not lost. You know who you are; keep focusing on that at all times. It is of the utmost importance that you stay focused at all times. Much love and gratitude to you.

Sunday, September 30, 2007

Greetings Nancy! We are so glad to be communicating with you again. This silence is not doing you or us any good at this time. It is imperative that you meditate. This is only setting back our goals. This also goes for Dan. We feel your frustration but as before, we assure you this frustration will be worth the rewards you both reap in the end. Please, the two you, have a great rest tonight and start fresh tomorrow. That is all. We admire you both for the tremendous effort you have put forth this far. Love to all.

Sunday, October 7, 2007

Greetings Nancy! Such a fine time; much happening now. We know you feel it; the uneasiness, the aches, the pains, but also the expansion of your mind. All is well; ride the waves of uneasiness with grace and everlasting faith. You know you must experience these hardships to get to the truth of who you really are. What a magnificent ride! The stars watch and cheer you on, child. Both you and Dan are a constant wonder to us; you have far surpassed our highest expectations. Thank you to both of you. We see this as an unprecedented success already. Much love to you both. Keep forging ahead, our earthly warriors.

Wednesday, October 10, 2007

Greetings Nancy! Why do you insist on working overtime? It is not in your best interests to do so at this time. Do not worry about your financial situation; all is taken care of. We know you want extra money; it will come in due time. Right now, we need you working with us for a brighter tomorrow. Do not worry about taking classes right now; they are not doing you or us any benefit at this time. Yes, you are speaking to the light beings; no other is allowed to penetrate your vibration. Please try to meditate more; we need you as much as you need us. Everything is still going as planned; and yes, you are still White Buffalo Calf Woman. We love you always.

Sunday, October 14, 2007

Greetings Nancy! Your duties as White Buffalo Calf Woman have already begun! Do you not think the natives who have met you have put two and two together? Remember who you are dealing with. They are more in touch with what is going on in the world than most others. Baby steps, remember for now, baby steps. Everything will unfold in due time. Xmas will soon be upon you; have fun! We know this is your FAVOURITE time of year. Enjoy yourselves; be in the moment. We will take care of the rest. That is all for now; many blessings to you and Dan.

Tuesday, October 16, 2007

Greetings Nancy! Staying at home right now is for the best. You are going through many changes right now; not all for the best. You must realign yourself mentally, physically and spiritually. This is the reason you feel "off" lately. Your spiritual side is taking a beating as of late; you have been very disconnected. Please remedy this as it is of the utmost importance. Still much to be done in a short period of time but all is still well. Rest your mind and get plenty of meditation. Your sleep is very disrupted right now due to added pressure inside your sub-conscious mind. This will be the norm for awhile. Just quiet your mind at times; this is good for your soul. Many blessings and love to you at this time.

Sunday, October 21, 2007

Greetings Nancy! You are most welcome for the feather. Now the real work begins. You see, we told you we would let you know when that would be. The feather signifies the time is here. Now don't get overly too excited; still dealing with baby steps here but the time is now. You will notice things happening now; people coming to you, places to go. Remember, baby steps. Such a grand exciting time. Blessings to you and Dan. Good luck and have fun. We are ever near to help; just call.

Sunday, October 28, 2007

Greetings Nancy! Well done! Many changes still taking place. We have done much work this week; the reason for your lack of energy and disconnectedness. Hang in there; it is almost complete. We know you are anxious to get on with it but timing is everything. Stay strong; keep on course. We feel your tension at work; all part of your learning. As we have told you before, we will bring people forward to you; you do not have to seek them out. You will, without a word of a doubt, know who they are immediately. You will not have to second guess yourself. This learning will continue on for awhile; remember, this is a year of learning for you. Year 2008, the master plan begins. Look forward with joy and bliss and know in your heart, you will truly be a miracle to all you meet. Everyone will be in awe and will hang on to your every word. This is how the world will change for the better. We love you dearly and wait patiently for your transformation. Love and blessings.

Saturday, November 3, 2007

Greetings Nancy! Yes, that was a gift we gave you last night. It was not for you to be there but we transpired all circumstances so you could see him. We feel your frustration at not being able to attend but it is not yet time to do so. It will happen in due time. We all love and miss you dearly. Your earthly life has been quite an adventure, has it not? You have been asking how your transformation is getting on and we are here to tell you everything is happening brilliantly; better than ever expected. You are a miracle; even to us in the higher realms. Yes, he knows where you are and knows it is not yet time for a meeting. News travels fast in the native community; even over two countries. The news of your attendance at this years powwows has traveled far and wide. Oh, the talk! If only you could hear. Much excitement and hope for a better tomorrow. Your existence has been a long awaited prophecy come true. Know that and be uplifted at the wonderful opportunities coming your way. Just believe in yourself; that is all. We love you, our tiny warrior. Dream big!

Tuesday, November 6, 2007

Greetings Nancy! Such wonderment! Even from where we are, we feel the excitement. Now is the time to focus on extremely positive thoughts. It is imperative. Always go about your day and have fun. That is all. We love you. Many blessings.

Friday November 9, 2007

Greetings Nancy! You have finally started the book! We have been waiting, and yes, we are helping you. All you have to do is ask. You know it's going to be a best seller, don't you? Everyone will want to know about your life before you "came out", so to speak. Yes, you will be going to Lake Louise soon. What a wonderful setting to continue writing your book in. Archangel Michael's energy is all around and so much easier to connect with him. You WILL, literally, have him on your back! Just ride the winds of change for now. Rest up and be prepared for a totally new tomorrow. We love you, dear one.

Tuesday, November 13, 2007

Greetings Nancy! Much going on. Please keep on top of your weight. We know it is difficult but we know you will succeed. The energy is now building to a faster climax; we know you can feel it. Just do what you are doing, think positive thoughts and watch what you're eating. Remarkable events will be occurring at a faster rate of speed. Be ready and enjoy! You and Dan deserve it. Much love to you both.

Tuesday, November 20, 2007

Greetings Nancy! It has been a week since our last communication. Time speeding up now. You have been so brave to come through such a trying adventure. No one else could have done what you have. Your many friends here wish you well on your new venture. Not long now. It will be very soon. We wish you to look back over the last year to see how far you have come. It will only get better. Rest up, dear one. Life is going to get a little hectic. You can do it. We have faith.

Tuesday, November 27, 2007

Greetings, dear one! Yes, we are here and we hear you. You are asking about your guides leaving so abruptly. You must remember, they have Not left. They aren't in the pyramid or in the garden but that doesn't mean they aren't with you, dear child. The reason behind this is because you are ready for the next stage. We have told you before; wonderful things will be happening. We feel your excitement over the powwow; we cannot imagine the sort of excitement that will be exhibited over what is next to come. You are on a great plateau waiting for everyone to catch up to you. But they won't; you are the leader, the teacher, the wise one. You must now set the example for others. Shine on, dear one. This is your ride. Love and blessings from all.

Saturday, December 1, 2007

Greetings, dear one! We are here and present at this time of wonderment. Shine for all to see. We, too, feel the excitement of the day. Blessed be to all who enter the realm of the Rogers Centre today! Spirits unite. A grand day for all. This is the start of something huge. And so the story begins. Blessings, dear one.

Sunday, December 2, 2007

Greetings, dear one! Much love and support to you at the powwow. Sometimes the greatest things that happen to one are unknown at the time. This is how it was for you. Don't worry; you were there to be seen and you were. That is what is important at this time; to be seen by others here and afar. Word has gotten out of your existence....many months ago. Yesterday, many from far away regions experienced light, love and spirit emanating all around you. Many are now wondering, "Is the prophecy true? Can it be"? Remember, this is a hard story to sell. Many will go home and have much time to think. Some will talk to spirit and all will eventually come to the same conclusion. "Yes, she is powerful. We know what we saw. My goodness, it must be so." Dear one, we know to you it was a disappointing powwow to say the least. Believe us, when we tell you, it was a complete success in the spirit world. All congratulate you for being you. Shine on, dear one. The success story will be yours. Blessings to you. And many blessings to Dan for his gentle nudges in the right direction.

Tuesday, December 11, 2007

Greetings from above! We are Many. We call ourselves this as we are too numerous to mention. We wish to speak through you. In this time of great turmoil, all must come to the realization of who they are. Too many missed opportunities going by. The masses must unite and this must begin now. This time of turmoil must be controlled. We wish to help in this matter. Further communiqués to follow soon. Thank you for your time.

Friday, December 14, 2007

Greetings from many. We and others like us, have been around since your planets creation. We know it is hard for you to understand but we move through timelines and have now found you. You are a very gentle person and you give off a very peaceful energy. You are good for this time and place and will be a force to reckon with. We wish to stay and watch this great dream unfold. We come in peace and are not here to harm or interfere. As we have said, we are Many and wish to help you along on your journey. Once again, thank you for your time.

Saturday, December 15, 2007

Hello from Many and all! We are happy to see you take down our messages of peace and goodwill. As we have mentioned previously, we are Many; time travelers extraordinaire. We have been to many universes and to many planets, but none so fascinating as this planet you call Earth. From our vantage point here, we can see she is in extreme decay. If something is to be done to save her, it must be now. We cannot stress this enough. We see that soon you will be entering the "teaching" phase of your journey. We wish to help with this. It is imperative that you reach many souls. We would like to work with those who are helping at this time. Thank you. Do not give up on your dreams…they are huge and so is your soul. You have much to offer others and will be a positive force for all who come in contact with you. You have asked about us; some are in solid form such as yourself. Others are a collective of energy not seen by the human eye but can definitely be felt. They will work through you to lift everyone's vibration; something that is required at this time. Thank you for letting us speak this day.

Sunday, December 16, 2007

Hello once again! We are so sorry to be taking up so much of your time but we are excited to be communicating with you. It is imperative that we talk. We see that you are expecting abundance in the form of money. We do not see that happening at this time. This is not the year for that to take place but it will come in due time. We see you have been waiting patiently and wish to tell you of this truth. In the universe, there is a special time and place for everything of importance to take place. We only ask for your patience in this matter. We see it is the holiday season and wish the best. Just remember, it will happen in due course. Once again, it is an honour to speak with you.

Monday, December 17, 2007

Hello from Many! We have been getting accustomed to this density of your world. You people really amaze us. We do not know how you function in this sluggish environment. Human beings are amazing creatures. One person so different from the next. We see your energy, light and love levels greatly diminish while you are at work. You do not like this environment, do you? Why not leave and teach? Teach what you know. You will soon remember. It is a slow process but it is coming. We can help you put together some lessons to teach. We are more than happy to help in this matter. When you are ready, just ask. We would be delighted to shine some different thoughts and awaken others to what is around and out in this massive universe that surrounds your earth. We are absolutely delighted to be here at this time; during this great awakening. Thank you for your time.

Sunday, December 22, 2007

Greetings from Many! Time speeding up, energy rising and bending out of shape for many on your planet. We see this next year as very chaotic for many. Your job now will be to come out and try to save humanity from self destruction. This time of woe has been in the cards for many millennia. It will seem as though a curse has been settled over earth like a blanket. We do not like to be the bearers of bad news but we wish you to be prepared. Take this time to rest your body, mind and spirit as you will be called upon next year to begin the teachings. That is all for now. We are sorry of the negativity of this communiqués but out of the dark must come the light. Happy Holidays to you both.

Wednesday, December 26, 2007

Yes, hello Nancy. It is I, Ashtar. Time has passed since we last spoke. I feel sadness for the emotions you are going through but it had to be this way. There is no sense in prolonging the inevitable. Soon enough, Christmas will make no sense to you so better to cut it off now. As much as you try to deny who you are or what your mission is, you know in your heart who you are. It matters not if you meditate; at least to us. You must realize you are only hurting yourself. This is your quiet time; time to get away from the pressures and densities of where you reside at this time. You knew, beforehand, this mission was not going to be easy. We knew you were the one for the job. We realize it is hard for you, in all that density, to keep a positive outlook all the time. Right now, you are going through a period of denial. Denial of who you are and a denial of what is happening in the big picture. It is O.K. to have these feelings; don't punish yourself. Deal with your emotions. Don't fluff them off. Take time to take care. There is no rush. You have just been through a rough time. If you need to talk about it, talk. If you need to shout, then shout. Don't hold in your emotions.

You must heal. In this next year, you will be called upon to start your mission. It is imperative to let go of your "human traits" and begin to show the world who you really are. So for now, rest and heal. It is for the betterment of humanity. Take care, our little warrior. Blessings.

YEAR 2008

Sunday, January 13, 2008

Greetings Nancy! Yes, it is I, Ashtar. Many beings surround you at this time, not all with the same belief system as you or I. Please, learn to discern between the two. You have had one in your dreamtime; please ignore him. There is nothing or no one who needs to teach you what you already know in your heart. Your time is soon; you feel it, the change that is coming. Be prepared for a joyous reunion.!! In answer to your question, no, you are based where you are and will stay as so. Yes, you will influence the masses; the how is still being kept a secret for now. Just take one day at a time and live in the moment. Take time, when you are alone, to reflect. Housework can always be done; take time to rest. All is well and on track for a joyous success. Blessings to you and Dan.

Saturday, January 26, 2008

Greetings Nancy! It is I, Ashtar. So glad we are in tune again. It has been a long journey, has it not? Not all roses, but you have learned much. I have directed you to an audio tape I wish for you to use on a daily basis. It is of the utmost importance. Not all experiences will be easy. Remember, just pass the darkness is the light. You must have a complete healing before you can go forward on your journey. All is well, wee one, for a fantastic lift-off. Sweet dreams and journey on.

Tuesday, January 29, 2008

Yes Nancy, I am here. Much happening at this time; seeming to come at you from all directions. It was to be and will eventually turn out for the better. He has some growing up to do and is being pushed to take his rightful path. You must look after yourself emotionally and physically. To do so is to stay on your own journey. Accept who you are and the healing will begin. Whenever you need me, I am always near. Blessings, dear one.

Thursday, January 31, 2008

Greetings Nancy! Ah…..you've come to the conclusion that the dream was of yourself. Good deduction. Will you be a believer now? Will you let others at work continue to walk all over you? They sense something about you and don't know if they like it or not. You will succeed at whatever you want to do. Be inspirational! Blessings!

Monday, February 11, 2008

Greetings Nancy! You are living proof that miracles happen. Enjoy! We have been watching from afar and agree that the time is NOW! This is Ashtar speaking once again. The command agrees with you that "Yes, it is time". We will be in constant contact with you over the next while helping you to get through a few hurdles. Don't be afraid; all is well. The world is waiting for you and they won't be let down. You have so much love in your heart and wish to help others in need. You know this is your life path. White Buffalo Calf Woman, you wear your title well. Be strong and proud. Blessings.

Thursday, February 14, 2008

Greetings Nancy! Ashtar here! We are so pleased with the progress you are making. You cannot as yet see the changes but we notice. Keep walking the straight path; all is well and on time. Believe in who you are; you know the truth and soon everyone will know. Don't hide; that is all. Blessings, dear one.

Friday, February 15, 2008

Greetings Nancy! Ashtar here. One minor thing we forgot to discuss yesterday. The tapes are wonderful to listen to but they are not going to tell you who you are; once again, you know in your heart. That is all. Blessings.

Tuesday, February 26, 2008

Greetings Nancy! Back to work tomorrow; do some more reflecting today. The time is very near. Raise your arms and heart in anticipation for it is to be. You are ready and so is the world. That is all. Peace be to you.

Friday, March 7, 2008

Greetings Nancy! All is well. How have you been? Well…we know. This is Many, once again. Progress is being made; you can feel it. Your time at work is almost at an end. You have made quite a difference you know; don't be mistaken. You have not even made a dent in what you will achieve. Looking to exciting times ahead. We are with you. Thank you for your time.

Thursday, March 13, 2008

Greetings Nancy! You're not feeling well and your foot hurts; all in a days work! Final adjustments are being made at this time and your body is going through a rejection period. All will be well; do not worry. That is all.

Monday, March 17, 2008

Greetings Nancy! Ashtar here. Once again, dear one, you are holding back. Yes, you are who you think you are. That has been revealed to you on numerous occasions and you know it to be the truth in your heart. Accept it. You know, as well as I, that the time is here to begin you're new life. Your place of employment was but a stepping stone to get you where you are now. You have much work ahead of you, so rest up now. It will soon be over, this hesitation about whether you should be at work or not. Does it not feel right to you being away from that place? You know you feel much more at peace. You can feel this peace all the time, you know. Very, very soon. Yes, the decision is yours to make but we will very soon make it very obvious to you. Yes, people will come to you. Maybe one has shown up already? Are you focusing on who's around you? Did Dan bring a message to you? An "aha" moment! You have many around you, just focus. The answers are there. Yes, you can get answers through meditation. Are you asking the questions? I am glad to see you have stayed home; you really do need this time. Please use it wisely. Housework can wait. Please focus and the answers will become so obvious you will wonder why you never saw them before now. Just rest, meditate and focus. All is well, our little warrior!

Yes Nancy, I am here. I know how you feel but this person does not matter right now. He does not figure into any of this, so his feelings at this time should be of no concern. You MUST focus on yourself, not someone else. This is what this day is all about; finding answers for you, not worrying about someone else's reactions. This is your time; use it wisely, dear one. The time is now; people are depending on you.

Don't worry about that at this time. When it is time for you to prove to people of who you are, you will have something to show. Nancy, this is needless worrying. Please, child, just focus on the here and now and everything else will fall into place with ease. You will see; I speak the truth.

Yes, if you want, I will bring a person to you, externally from work who will say, "I am suppose to work with you". Then you must keep your end of the bargain. And it is so.

Tuesday, April 1, 2008

Greetings Nancy! Focus! We are here to tell you it doesn't matter much anymore how tired you are now; your days of having to work are numbered. The intensity of the situation is getting stronger and the world is waiting. As far as having a past life regression, you can have one but you won't get much more out of it than you already know in your heart. It will give you the confirmation you so greatly need. Hang in there. The time is NOW. We love you. The Council.

Saturday, April 5, 2008 (Light-beings)

Greetings Nancy! The time is now; there is magic in the air, is there not? You feel it on many levels. Are you ready for the responsibility? We feel that you are but you must also feel it in your heart. There will be no turning back. We played this song for a reason; to relay to you the magnificence of the situation. People are now coming into place. You will soon see evidence of this and the beauty of the situation. We are forever here to help. Blessings to you. We have much admiration and respect for you on this journey; the journey of a lifetime. We love you.

Saturday, April 19, 2008

Greetings Nancy! Ashtar here! So good to hear from you! Yes, I can help with the small dilemma you find yourself in. Sometimes the heart has been known to flip-flop back and forth between one side of the question to the other. Is this the answer or that the answer? Of course, you know of free will and that we, of the higher realms, can only guide you. As in before, I have explained about following your heart, but in this case when you are so unsure, I will give you a few pointers to ponder. There are different forms of paganism; there are those that worked with the land…knew about plant life; could mix herbal remedies, watched the animals and learned from them. They also watched the moon and the stars and at one time were called witches. There are also those who follow the fairy, gnome and pixie kingdom in the elementals. And yes, the native american culture is pagan. Which categories do you fall into? I hope you're thinking "all" because you do. You are from the stars, you follow the native spirituality and you also love the elemental kingdom. The choice is up to you to go to the pagan-fest; no big deal. Make your moccasins and dance your heart out or have a quiet weekend at home. Your choice! I hope this little discussion has settled your heart. Be brave, our little warrior! Lots of love from above.

Thursday, April, 24, 2008

Greetings Nancy! Ashtar here! Mercury is rising and so are you! There is a stirring in the air wherever you go…a few have felt it today. It is a day of truths; people are drawn to you and Dan. This is just the start of the excitement. There is more to follow; just keep a clear mind and your feet to the earth. My brave ones, go forward in glory. Blessings to you both!

Saturday, April 26, 2008

Greetings Nancy! Thank you for moving forward. Planting sweet grass and sage; ceremony is very important. Never lose touch with your reality. Your native guides are very happy this day. Much love.

Saturday, May 3, 2008

Greetings Nancy! Ashtar here with the latest news from the stars. We watch over you day and night; there is no need to worry. Just be at one with yourself. We tell you the time is drawing ever near; you feel the anticipation and also the fear of the unknown. DO NOT WORRY! Keep a calm mind and heart; we are ever present. Stay focused on your goal; it is your truth. Blessings.

Sunday, May 4, 2008

Greetings Nancy! The Command thanks you and Dan for planting the stones! Watch the manifestation take place now! Much excitement, here and there. The right ones will walk into your life now at this time. Trust and believe. Blessings to you both.

Friday, May 9, 2008

Greetings Nancy! I tried to contact you; a frightening experience but now I know what frequency to use. Next time will be a success. This is Ashtar and the Command, looking forward to our meetings. Till next time, my friend. Blessings.

Date Unknown

Greetings Nancy. So much going on right now; not to worry, everything is fine. Ashtar here. Dan is finally putting two and two together and coming up with White Buffalo Calf Woman. Good for him. You see, it is time. Many experiences happening now; just go with the flow. Everything is fine and right on time. We know you have many aches and pains and feelings of "lack of energy", but these too shall pass. All part of the process. Not to worry. We watch and wait. Blessings to you, our little warrior.

Date Unknown

Greetings Nancy! The Wise Ones will soon arrive; work hard, work faithfully; all is well. Most of your emotions you are dealing with at this time are due to the intensity of energy at this time. Be well; look after yourself. Blessings.

Wednesday, June 4, 2008

Greetings Nancy! Ashtar here. Wanting to give you a few days to get your mind use to the idea of not having to exist in such a negative space. Congratulations! This, the time both you and we, of the Command, have waited some time for. A little rest now for you and everything will start gung-ho very soon. Rest your mind now; all is well and looked after. Recuperate, for soon the teachings will begin in earnest. We, of the Command, applaud you. Blessings.

Sunday, June 8, 2008

Greetings Nancy! We are One here! We want to ask you to guard your thoughts; you are on the verge of a big break-through. You have come a long way to have everything go topsy-turvy now. We know you can succeed and pull this off. Who are you? Who do you tell us you are? That is all. Blessings.

Ho, greetings from Chiefs! Things went well yesterday. You were tired and unprepared for all the energy. Better days ahead. We were with you, heating up the drums! People are drawn to you; they don't make it obvious. That is the way. Have fun and keep smiling; your smile can light up the world. Megwich!

Greetings Nancy! Ashtar here. Think positively, do positively, live positively. All will be well. The Wise Ones are who you think and have the knowledge of which you seek. It can be yours also; just concentrate. Give light, give love. No holding back! This world is your oyster. Take care of all. Blessings.

Wednesday, June 18, 2008

Greetings Nancy! So good to talk with you since it has been, shall we say, quite awhile. This is St. Germaine speaking. It is my honour to welcome you back into the fold. You have played the game well. Portions have lasted well beyond the time expected. Bravo to you! As you can see, your game has taken an abrupt turn. We have had to implement this as we were well afraid your game was going to continue even further. Sometimes we don't know where you get the willpower to continue on the same journey. This change in your lifestyle was orchestrated by us as we were told by you to interfere on your behalf if things were getting out of control. Rest is needed to get rid of the cobwebs in your mind. Too many years of beating down negativity and unrest. One soul can only handle so much. Your visions will come to fruition but only with some hard work on your part. You must get more exercise as the weight must come off. This also goes for Daniel. We are very worried about his eating habits or eating disorder, shall I say. This also goes for you. More fruits and vegetables. Dairy and meat is not acceptable in large quantities, Dan. Once or twice a week is sufficient. You have a long road ahead, which can be cut in half, time wise if you start to adhere to these restrictions. That is all for now. Much love to you both. I will return.

Sunday, June 22, 2008

Greetings Nancy! One more day till the "big one"! Wonderful celebration yesterday! You were well received. The energy was wonderful! More to come! The excitement builds. Blessings to you both. "The Council"

Monday, June 23, 2008 7th Anniversary Day!

Greetings, dear one! We, from the higher dimensions, wish to congratulate you both on your 7th anniversary. We wish all the best to you both. Things are well and the excitement builds. Thank you for exercising; you are both making a solid effort and for that we thank you immensely. That is all for now. Keep well and much love.

Thursday, July 10, 2008

Greetings Nancy! Ashtar here. All is well. Just be at peace. Your time will come. Opportunity is shifting into place. Those who need to be near you at this time will start to show up in your life. You will know, without a shadow of a doubt, that they are to be there. Welcome them for it is to be so. Be prepared for an external shift in consciousness. At this time, please sit and talk with us on a daily basis. It is important. Thank you. Many blessings.

Friday, July 11, 2008

Greetings Nancy! Ashtar here, once again. There is much turmoil now; all for a reason. You are torn between stepping forward and taking charge or should you stand back and watch this scenario play out? Maybe there is a halfway point or median point that you can operate from. You should be there maybe for support but let others master their own lives. That is best. You have become well at mastering your own life; what will be, will be.

It is a hard lesson to learn, is it not? A lesson well learned. Just remember that everything happens as it should and for a reason. Thank you for, once again, having this connection with me. All is well. Blessings.

Saturday, July 12, 2008

Greetings Nancy! Such an upsetting start to the day but we knew you would make a good decision for yourself. Time spinning; one day into the next, never seeming to hesitate long. Your time coming faster than you know. Thank you for connecting once again. Blessings.

Sunday, July 13, 2008

Greetings Nancy! Ah yes, a revelation! Yes, we will be coming down on you as this is the time for serious study. Journeying, meditation, reading; all is important. Also, please get back out in nature; so important! Also, please, please sit out at night time and connect with the stars. You have so many willing and able to help. This is your path. Celebrate it! Blessings.

Monday, July 14, 2008

Greetings Nancy! I know you have been concerned with your left ear. Do not worry; we are fine tuning your hearing one ear at a time. It is uncomfortable but will be worth it in the long run. Thank you for informing me of the inner condition of the ear. I will try to remedy that. Also, thank you for delving into the shamanic reading; so many wondrous experiences for you. We know you enjoyed so much the journey with your guide and much more of those journeys are yet to come. We, of the higher realms, promise you this. I am most proud of your accomplishments thus far. You may not see this, but you have come so far since the end of May. Keep straight and true. Blessings.

Tuesday, July 15, 2008

Greetings, dear one! Ashtar here. We are gently guiding you forward on your journey. Your absolute ultimate goal is within your grasp. Gently take it and run. Do what your heart desires. It is yours for the taking. Blessings.

Wednesday, July 16, 2008

Greetings Nancy! All is well. Keep studying, it will be well worth it. Your financial abundance will come when it is needed. Look for amazing things to happen quite unexpectedly. Keep exercising. It is important. Blessings.

Thursday, July 17, 2008

Greetings White Buffalo Calf Woman! You have made it! Do you think you'll be able to stand the excitement? I hope so cause it's coming fast now. There's no stopping it! The celebration is going on up here. You can feel it. Once again....congratulations from all above. Blessings.

Friday, July 18, 2008

Greetings White Buffalo Calf Woman! Such a long name to write now instead of just writing Nancy. Ashtar here. It is time for your shamanic journey. All your questions will be answered. You have come such a long way and the time is here. That is all; longer discussions to come. Blessings.

Saturday, July 19, 2008

Greetings Nancy. Yes, it is Ashtar. You are becoming quick. You have noticed the name by which I have called you. Good work, White Buffalo

Calf Woman! Ah, it didn't take long. Time for a journey. Whenever you are ready. Many blessings!

Sunday, July 20, 2008

Greetings White Buffalo Calf Woman! It is Many, back to speak with you again. You are now at the final stage, where you step into your own. We are glad to see you have freed up some time in which to do your work. Thank you for that. We are honored to be in amongst your midst. We are here to help in whatever capacity you deem fit. Always with much honour. Blessings, dear one.

Blessings White Buffalo Calf Woman! Ashtar here. We hover over above but as yet have not seen you outside at nightfall. Why is this? You know at night we can make such a perfect connection. Weather permitting, please come out tonight. Thank you. Blessings.

Monday, July 21, 2008

Greetings Nancy. Ah…you've noticed again. Good for you! Thank You for being outdoors last evening and looking upwards. Did I not tell you I would show? Yes, White Buffalo Calf Woman, this is Ashtar speaking. I'm sorry I may have startled you this morning but sometimes we need a "not so gentle" nudge or two, do you not think? Something a little effective. If not, we may eat chips and watch TV. for a greater part of the day. That would be counter-productive for the work that you must do. Remember, everything in moderation. Soon…very soon. Blessings.

Tuesday, July 22, 2008

Greetings White Buffalo Calf Woman! Such a busy day; all working out well. Never, ever fear. Yes, once in awhile difficult circumstances appear, but we must work through them. You came through your journey yesterday with but a scratch. Keep journeying! As always, many blessings.

Wednesday, July 23, 2008

Greetings White Buffalo Calf Woman! Ashtar here. We, of the Council, applaud you in your caring of others. To have such devotion to a four-legged member of your family; so much so that you are up practically the whole night through. She is lucky to have such devoted guardians as you and Daniel. She knows that she is well loved. Many blessings; Ashtar here, signing off.

Thursday, July 24, 2008

Greetings, dear one. Many here. We wish to speak with you today. Have you decided to go into business? It will be very profitable and the people you will need will come. You only have to have an affirmative answer in your head and it is so, you see. Sometimes the answer is in the phone. Ah, The Heart Centre. With a name such as this, how can it be anything but positive. Ideas will come to you; open your mind. Thank you for your time. Blessings to one and all.

Greetings White Buffalo Calf Woman! Energy spinning, spinning. Things are happening. Go with the flow. Exercise and energy go hand in hand. It can all be accomplished, just focus! That is all, focus. Blessings.

Friday, July 25, 2008

Greetings White Buffalo Calf Woman! Such a wonderful day to be outdoors. The time is soon and you must get used to a different lifestyle. That is all. Ashtar signing off. Blessings.

Saturday, July 26, 2008

Greetings White Buffalo Calf Woman! Yes, we the Council are from the light. Please journey upwards so we may speak. You are always safe. It is time for you to know your mission. Thank you and blessings.

Tuesday, July 29, 2008

Greetings White Buffalo Calf Woman! Ashtar here. So good to connect with you again! So much has happened since our last communiqué. Several portals around your property are now activated. Look to phenomenal happenings skywards! Do not despair because you did not think you connected with us, the Council. We were there right with you. Your vision and hearing will improve. Did I not tell you we were adjusting your hearing, and your left ear does not bother you anymore for the most part. The same will happen with your vision. Someday you may not need your glasses anymore. Would you like that? So, see, everything is improving; it just takes time. And time is all we have. Make the most of your "downtime" because this too will not last. If you want to teach, you will teach. And teach you must. Your "peeps" as you call them, need you. Also, adjustments needed on your spine, therefore a sore back for a few days. We will talk again tomorrow. Blessings to you.

Wednesday, July 30, 2008

Greetings White Buffalo Calf Woman! It is I, Ashtar! Feeling a little housebound? First, tired of work; now tired of relaxation. I know you do not miss work, but please, I wish you would know you are looked after. Things will happen when it is time. Take a deep breath and settle down. Everything is O.K. Just relax and take time for yourself. Blessings.

Thursday, July 31, 2008

Greetings White Buffalo Calf Woman! Ashtar here! I want to tell you it is within you to see the light; to see your true self. The harmonic convergence, 8.8.8 will bring about significant change in you and your surroundings. Look beyond that which is right in front of you; you can do this. It will come. Meditate and keep in contact with us while doing your chores over the next few days. You are shining so bright now; don't forget your protection. Please sit outdoors at night. It is important. Blessings.

Sunday, August 3, 2008

Greetings White Buffalo Calf Woman! Ashtar here! Good turnout for the powwow yesterday. So much went on that you have no idea about. All is good. The awakening will be soon and quick. Then there will be no more questions. Until then, no worrying; have fun. Blessings.

Monday, August 4, 2008

Greetings White Buffalo Calf Woman! Many here. We have come to you, this eve, to ask you to take charge of what is in your heart. You must search for the truth and you will be free. Honour yourself, honour Mother Earth, honour us. This is the way to move forward. Find yourself. Thank you for, once again, your time with us.

Greetings White Buffalo Calf Woman! Ashtar here! Never set aside thoughts that come to you and stay for they are divinely guided. Move forward; you are looked after. Don't waste your energy worrying; put it to good use finding your answers. They are there for the taking. You just have to search in your heart. Much love to you from myself and the command.

Tuesday, August 5, 2008

Greetings White Buffalo Calf Woman! Many here, once again. We wish to speak with you about matters of the heart. Are they real; are they make-believe, not existing at all? Only you can tell what is in your own heart, not someone else. If something is in the heart, it is like a fire burning within. If the fire is not there, there is no substance to that which you want to move forward with. So keep the fire lit; let it burn brightly for all to see. Then sit back and watch the magic happen! Just watch. Thank you for your time. Love from Many.

Greetings White Buffalo Calf Woman! Ashtar here. The only thing I wish to add is just focus and concentrate on what direction your life will take. Nothing is "too big"! Blessings.

Wednesday, August 6, 2008

Greetings White Buffalo Calf Woman! Ashtar here. Study and you will find the answers. Just do the research. All along the answers have been there but the timing has been wrong. Now is the time. It's in your heart, this truth. All the pieces will come together very nicely. The Command wishes you well. We are here if you need us. Blessings.

Friday, August 8, 2008

Greetings White Buffalo Calf Woman! Ashtar and the Command welcome you. To you, we are but a thought in your mind, some intangible belief that is eons away; yet here we are communicating. That is the brilliance of this whole story; for it is the now, this minute, that you seek. You are the story; only you will unlock the teachings. When you find your key, you will find your teachings. Be brave and look. It is there. We are always here to assist. Blessings.

Saturday, August 9, 2008

Greetings White Buffalo Calf Woman! Ashtar here. We know your heart and soul hungers to create. The mission is simple; it always has been. To remember, that is all. It will come to you, soon. Blessings.

Monday, August 11, 2008

Greetings White Buffalo Calf Woman! Ah, the key. Simple wasn't it? Yes, that was it all this time. Ashtar here. So we've found the key, let the rest of the story begin. A snap, snap, snap of the fingers; it will be that fast. You have waited patiently for the most part. Now relax and feel refreshed that things will start to happen, people will start to appear. Congratulations; much clapping and sighs of relief over here. Blessings.

White Buffalo Calf Woman. Many here with many wishes of luck and good fortune for you. You inspire us in so many ways. Never give up on your dreams. We greatly admire you. Thank you for your time.

Blessings to our White Buffalo Calf Woman! Sitting Bull, Red Cloud and Broken Arm here. See, it was so simple. A white feather for your medicine pouch. You were given a headdress full of white feathers sometime ago.; that was your first clue to the importance of the "White Feather. Wear it and breath it into your very being, your soul. You are in our heart.

Tuesday, August 12, 2008

Greetings White Buffalo Calf Woman! Many here, wishing to communicate with you once again. Your fear is of not having enough; not having the freedom of knowing the cash is there for the bills. We are here to tell you there is so much money around you right now that you can almost reach out and touch it. As you know, the lottery is not the only way to gain abundance. Do not project the vibes of "not having enough". Everything is on track for a great success. You have all the abundance you need and more. Relax and think positive. Thank you for your time.

Greetings White Buffalo Calf Woman. Ashtar here. You are so close; just keep positive. Ah, it will be a grand journey! And, of course, we will be there to cheer you on. The pot of gold awaits, dear one. Blessings.

Wednesday, August 13, 2008

Greetings White Buffalo Calf Woman! Many here. This message you received this morning was from the collective energy of Many. We wish to have direct contact with you and will come in a non-threatening way. Yes, we are from the light, so no worries about that; but it is good that you ask. You are well protected. Thank you, once again, for your time.
White Buffalo Calf Woman, the Council here. At this moment we are the energies of Ashtar, Sananda and St, Germaine. We shall be present along with the energies of Many. This shall be a meeting of great inspiration for you. You shall benefit in such a way that you will know your purpose and about how to execute it. It is all good; no worries. Blessings, dear one and happy dreams.
Your guides are always near.

Thursday, August 14, 2008

Greetings White Buffalo Calf Woman. Many here. Yes, we are from the light. We wish to thank you for taking this trip. We know this is out of the ordinary for you; just picking up and taking off for a much-needed vacation. The energies of Lake Louise are good for you. Expect great things to materialize on this trip. This is only the beginning of something big. Thank you for your time. It has been our pleasure.
Ah, White Buffalo Calf Woman. You are coming home! Ashtar here. You seem puzzled. You have many ties to Lake Louise; most of yet to be found. Michael is waiting for your visit to "his turf". Just relax and enjoy the trip. See you there! Blessings!

Friday, August 15, 2008

Greetings White Buffalo Calf Woman! Many here, with greetings of goodness and of thinking positively. We see a lot of worrisome energy around you; we understand, but really, not to worry. There will be nothing to be frightened of. After your trip, you will return home with a much clearer state of mind. You will know what your purpose is. We wish to tell you though, because both you and Daniel are highly enlightened, you will see things that you are not used to. Do not be afraid, all is well. We tell you this as it is hard to work with you surrounded with an energy full of fear. Just try to breathe deeply and stay calm, both of you. All is well. Lord Michael will be present. Thank you for your time.
White Buffalo Calf Woman! Ashtar here. Nothing much to add on to what Many has spoken to you today of. All is well, in fact you may find it quite amusing. We shall see you in a few days. Blessings.

Sunday, August 17, 2008

Dear White Buffalo Calf Woman! Please get some sleep tonight; you are too stressed out. We really cannot work with you this way. Many here. Your energy is depleted. You need your light. Too much time on the road. Please get rest and exercise. Thank you for your time.
White Buffalo Calf Woman, Ashtar here! Please try to stay calm. All is not lost. Tomorrow is another day. Chin up! Blessings.

Tuesday, August 19, 2008

Dear White Buffalo Calf Woman! You see, not everything turns out as planned. This is not the way of your world. There are many twists and turns but in this case, everything turned out o.k. You have to learn to ride with the tide and make the best of every situation. That is all that is expected; nothing more, nothing less. Rest up for tomorrow. Thank you for your time.

White Buffalo Calf Woman, Michael speaking. You are here and that is always good. Shall we chat again tomorrow? Find some seclusion, please, away from the crowds. Thank you.

Wednesday, August 20, 2008

Dear White Buffalo Calf Woman! Michael here. I am so glad the rain did not deter you. Isn't it beautiful here? A little bit of paradise here on earth. We will talk later in quiet. Blessings.

We are here. We are Many and we've been walking around you disguised as humans. We wish to see what it is like. The air is so heavy in your atmosphere. We won't be staying long. Thank you for spreading your light.

Saturday, August 23, 2008

Greetings White Buffalo Calf Woman! Many here. You will start to see things change at a very rapid speed now. You are now in the planning stage and that is what we like to see. Keep moving forward; magic awaits. Play the game; look for more clues you will understand. Thank you, again.

Ashtar here. You are holding up well. Ah… the grand reunion of the seven. Didn't I speak a while back of the reunion everyone is waiting for? Now you know. Keep the faith. Blessings.

Sunday, August 24, 2008

Greetings White Buffalo Calf Woman! You are back home now and once again worrying of money problems; please don't do this. Many speaking. Please keep a positive attitude; you are so close now. One day at a time; just take one day at a time and do your planning. Ideas will flow. We know you are tired from your trip so get plenty of rest. Think positive; all is well. Thank you for your time.

White Buffalo Calf Woman, Ashtar here. So glad to be, once again, in contact with you. You will have plenty of opportunity, in the next few days, to do some planning. You know your dreams are coming to fruition; ah, seven sisters, now there's a story to be told. You will figure it all out. Blessings.

Thursday, August 28, 2008

Dear White Buffalo Calf Woman. Many here. We have not had a very good communication since you returned home from your trip. Do not beat yourself up over the thoughts that may come to you as a result of things not going perfectly in your day. Turn the thought around and just learn something from it. The vehicle will be ready tomorrow in time for "uncle". We are glad to see you are a little on the creative side today. This is good. As far as you knowing your mission…all in good time. You are not quite ready yet and neither is the world. Don't worry of your financial situation; we will look after it, to give you both a break. The minds need rest from everyday trivial matters. Rest and get strong. Believe us, you will need every iota of strength you have to do what must be done. All good. Thank you for your time.
White Buffalo Calf Woman, Ashtar here. We come from above to constantly stay in contact with you. These writings are not in vein and will someday go down in history! There is more going on in the background than meets the eye and miracles and magic do happen. Keep this in mind. Blessings.

Friday, August 29, 2008

Greetings White Buffalo Calf Woman! Many here with greetings of joy. We see your light shining from so far away. The love you give to others is phenomenal. Keep shining and do enjoy yourself tonight. Thank you for your time.

Ashtar here. Glad tidings to you; all is well. To say more would defeat the purpose. Many blessings.

Greetings White Buffalo Calf Woman. Michael here. I hear your thoughts of the lack of knowledge of the purpose of your mission. You know who you are and soon you will know what to teach others and how to go about this. Timing…it's all just down to timing. Thank you.

Sunday, August 31, 2008

Greetings White Buffalo Calf Woman! Many here. We wish to tell you of the teachings of today. Not all will sit well with you, that is O.K.; just believe what is in your own heart for the good of all mankind. All is well… uncle is good…you will know him well. So many possibilities exist for you right now. Look to the skies and always believe what you see, for it is your truth. Thank you for your time.

Greetings White Buffalo Calf Woman, Ashtar here. Good day today; part of the prophecy is being filled this weekend. Be strong, dear one, for this is the start of the rest of the prophecy to come. Blessings.

Friday, September 5, 2008

Greetings White Buffalo Calf Woman! Many here. Yes, of course you may speak with us every day. If you are extremely busy some days and cannot do so, that is also alright. No fixed rules on communication, although, if something does come up and you do hear your ears ringing, please communicate with us as soon as possible. Do not worry about being tired, this will come and go. We would like to see you visiting other dimensions more often. Thank you for your time.

Greetings White Buffalo Calf Woman! I would like to expand a little about looking to the stars. What you and Daniel saw the other day was, of course, one of our scout ships. You will be seeing these more often and in greater numbers. It is time we were seen by others also. This also is all part of the grand prophecy coming true. The more we come out, the more you will come out. So be it. Blessings.

October 14 Sighting?

Yes, this is our target date. In your location, you may not see the mother ship but will certainly see scout ships such as those you have seen before. This first major sighting date was not to be at this time but we have pushed the date ahead as per the conditions on your planet. This is Many and thank you for your time.

September 6, 2008 Identity of Many?

Greetings White Buffalo Calf Woman. Yes, we are the Galactic Federation of Light. Because you have linked us together and have asked us to show ourselves, this will take place as scheduled. Thank you for your time.

September 8, 2008

Greetings White Buffalo Calf Woman! The Federation here; we will be showing ourselves next month on the fourteenth day. Be sure of this. We, the Federation, have waited some time for this. As we have spoken of before, there is now too much corruption on your planet on many different levels. As we have stated, we come in peace and wish no harm to anyone. We only wish the masses to know of our existence. This time was also prophesized a long time ago in earth years. Others foretold of the many changes mother earth would experience at the hands of mankind. Now, it is time for us to soon assist in her cleansing. Your teachings will revolve around this. Many are starting to see there is more to you than the "outer package" per se. You have much to learn in the next while; please rest up. You are most welcome for your drum. She is your heartbeat combined with mother earth's, a very powerful being in herself. Thank you for your time.

Greetings White Buffalo Calf Woman! Ashtar here; we will soon see each other again. It has been awhile in your timeline. You will not recognize me but we are old friends, you and I. Daniel noticed one of us at the powwow this weekend. Good eyes, Daniel. You will remember him as the long haired bearded man sitting off to the side by himself. Sananda wears disguises well, does he not? I must say he thoroughly enjoyed himself. You and Daniel really commanded the grounds and he was proud to see you with your drum. Remember, when the
Student is ready, the teacher will come. Blessings.

Tuesday, September 9, 2008

Greetings White Buffalo Calf Woman! As soon as your partner Daniel comes home, please go outdoors and meld your heartbeat with Mother Earth's. Yes, this is the Federation. Ah, your drum is a beautiful being. She is very powerful. Together you will heal many. The ultimate purpose is to heal others and let them know your love. Remember, you are one of our representatives here on earth. Through you, they will know love and peace. Thank you for your time.
White Buffalo Calf Woman. Michael here. You know this is part of the prophecy coming true. You have come to my altar in the Rockies and now your drum has come home to you. It is time for you and the Federation to shine! Blessings!

Wednesday, September 10, 2008

Greetings White Buffalo Calf Woman! Many here, or should we say the Federation as you now know us by. We have come to speak of next months visit to your planet. Where you are situated, you will only see very little of the craft on your horizon. There will be some scout ships….not many as your government and military will try to disconnect the protective shields we will place around the ship. We promise, though, both you and Daniel will have contact with us. And so your teachings begin. Tell Daniel to

hold onto those thoughts as there are more to add on to those. We have contacted you as you were watching a video on your computer....we wish for you not to watch it at this time. What he says is true but for now we would rather you not get caught up in all the details. You need much rest....we cannot stress this enough. Your human form is going through so many changes right now that you cannot even begin to comprehend. Please rest, it is of the utmost importance. Thank you for your time.
Greetings White Buffalo Calf Woman! Ashtar here. On the 14th day of October you will visit with me. Of course, Daniel also. At this time, we wish to inform you of your earthly mission. After the three day period, when our ship has left your atmosphere, your missions will begin in earnest. I wish you to know of this. Prepare yourselves. Thank you. Blessings.

Thursday, September 11, 2008

Greetings White Buffalo Calf Woman! The Federation here. It has been quite a musical morning. We always like your choice of music. You were speaking of the 14th this morning with your friend. You do realize that you know him very well. Both of you are also good friends from another time and space, should we say. We, also, can be quite humorous. Back to the 14th. You say you can't imagine just how topsy-turvy everyone will be. Well, imagine the worst case scenario and times that by ten. For those of you on the planet that know of us, it won't be difficult. Unfortunately, a large part of your population does not; or does not believe in us. For those dear souls it will be complete bedlam. "Freaking out" is putting it mildly. The media really will have them believing that we are here for reasons other than the good of all mankind. Please try to keep those in your close vicinity calm. Reassure them that we mean no harm and that we are only here to educate the population. Thank you for your time.

Friday, September 12, 2008

Greetings White Buffalo Calf Woman! The Federation here once again; we wish to speak today of love, the universe and what is expected in the near future. Most everyone on your planet has done their very best to keep the light shining and to live an extraordinary, positive life…a life that has not brought another harm. You see, even these people will be greatly shaken with what they are about to see. It is one thing to think that there may be others in your universe but quite another to actually see evidence before their very eyes. That is where our messengers on earth come in…to spread the word that we mean no harm. The faster the word gets out, the less turmoil there will be. Yes, both you and Daniel will go on the road; that is a true fact. We have been watching your progress on the "world tour" planning. You have brought up many wonderful points and we will talk soon. Ah, our two dear warriors, soon, very soon, your veils shall be lifted and instantly you will remember everything. Will your role on earth be over? No, unless you want it to be for it will be your decisions. We hope your "world tour" will help you to stay grounded in your missions. White Buffalo Calf Woman, I am afraid you may have to go looking for this woman. She has not forgotten about you. She may phone, she may not. She is very intimidated by you and your drum. You see, dear one, this is what your life will be like now. Not many friends and unfortunately for both you and Daniel, not much in the way of family either. This is the way it was to be. We know you sense the distance already. They will be O.K. without you. We do not mean to sound so callous; it must hurt your hearts to have this happen. You must see, though, that you have a huge mission to accomplish that will take up a lot of your time. There are many beings, many galaxies that watch and wait, cheering you on, for dear ones, this dream is the dream of an entire lifetime for all, above and below. Thank you for your time.

Saturday, September 13, 2008

Greetings White Buffalo Calf Woman! This is the Federation of Light speaking. Irohol speaking. We wish you to look upon this day as one of many teachings from those around you, far and near. We wish you to not worry of the drum for she came to you, she is part of you and in time will be blessed. She would never come to you as a showpiece. Know this. Your earth days are ticking away; closer and closer to our journey to an "earth day" celebration. Have joy in your heart. Your friends of the stars miss you and cannot wait to connect with you again. Thank you for your time.

Sunday, September 14, 2008

Greetings White Buffalo Calf Woman! Ashtar here from the Federation of Light. One more of your earthly months to go until we all reunite again. Did we tell you that both you and Daniel are missed so much? We have such wonderful times together. It is going to be a reconnection of sacred souls. We do hope, however, you both stay grounded in your missions. From the 14th of October onwards, it will be much easier for you both as you will have direct contact with us whenever the need may arise. We are very busy here on the ship preparing our descent into your earth plane. The excitement is building here on board as I know both of you feel the same. We feel it from your hearts. Stay strong; time is quickening until that magical moment. Blessings.

Monday, September 15, 2008

Greetings White Buffalo Calf Woman! The Federation here. Solai here, with Ashtar. We wish to speak with you today of the mother ship. It takes quite a bit of work to descend a 200 mile long ship into your atmosphere. There are many modules that must be activated before we even begin the descent. Some of these modules have been laying dormant for some time. We also have to make sure all of our security shields are in place and in working order. We have begun this work in earnest. We are looking forward for this part of the prophecy to take place. Such exciting times! We see, as you write this communiqué from us, you are staring out the window and marveling at the blue skies. You are thinking "What a change from earlier in the day"! This is how fast one person's world can change. For all of humanity, the world is going to change drastically come next month. Lives will never be the same again. Do you like what you see out your window? The new world will be like this; shiny and new. So see, it's not really a high price to pay for the beauty, serenity, peace and love that will be the new earth. You'll see. Thank you for your time.

Thank you Ashtar and Solai.

Tuesday, September 16, 2008

Greetings White Buffalo Calf Woman! The Federation of Light here. Today there is a group of us present to speak our thoughts and ideas to you. First off, we would like to say that we are happy to see you writing once again. We see a bestseller in the works! Next, we would like to speak of family. We see you are worried about not seeing enough of them. This was foretold a while ago and is to be expected. If you wish to see them, we feel the weekends would be better, as at this time, it is best you have the quietness of your own home through the week. Writing is important at this time. You see, your book will be a teaching to others. A writer always thinks their words are not good enough. And yet, those very same people turn out works that sell, time and time again. Get the message? Don't let your own insecurities hold you back from telling your story. We are forever here to help. Just call on us. Thank you for your time.

Thank you Federation of Light.

Wednesday, September 17, 2008

Greetings White Buffalo Calf Woman! Yes, WE are the Federation. Thank you for sensing the difference in voice tone. May we say it is good to see you writing and typing. We tell you, "Just watch, it will be a seller". You see, everything could be tied in together. Going on the road, speaking and promoting your new book! That would all tie in nicely together, would it not? We are full speed ahead for the fourteenth of next month. Still a few things to iron out but all is on schedule for our decent to earth. We give you and Daniel our blessings and know we are looking forward to our reunion. Thank you for your time.

Thank you Federation

Thursday, September 18, 2008

Greetings White Buffalo Calf Woman! Ashtar here. You've had a very busy day; Mom and Dad appreciate your visit. They do miss you immensely. Really, not to much to discuss. Things still on target for next month. There are so many people here that want to see you again. You and Daniel are well missed. Your chairs on deck await you. Blessings and rest up for your next big adventure.

Thank you Ashtar

Friday, September 19, 2008

Greetings White Buffalo Calf Woman. This is the Galactic Federation of Light speaking. We know for awhile we have been coming to you as "many". At that time, we were not prepared to come forth as the Galactic Federation of Light because of past agreements between both you and the council. Now it is time for us to come forth as the Galactic Federation of Light. We previously called ourselves "many", as, really, that is who we are. We are many beings from many planets in many galaxies! We want to speak to you and Daniel today about what is happening with your physical bodies and minds. Daniel, first off, we wish to speak to you of the hardships you are experiencing right now due to the workplace. We wish to ask you at this time to "stick it out" until the fourteenth of next month. Nancy is experiencing some anxiety over this and we have to tell you at this time, your heartache is not anywhere near the level as Nancy's before she quit. Please Daniel, be the warrior you are during these last weeks. You probably remember a communiqué we previously sent, stating that we had to step in and intervene in behalf of Nancy....as our little warrior would have gone on working forever. She went on long past the time she should have quit working. We didn't exactly have forever to play out that scenario. Daniel, when you and Nancy come to the ship, we will discuss the next journey on earth. No, at that time you will no longer be associated with your workplace. But, at this time, you both will be given the opportunity to follow through with your mission or stay with us on the ship. If you continue your stay on earth, you can be rest assured that your life will be considerably easier (abundance wise) but will involve a lot of travel......weeks away from home and quite a grueling pace to keep. We wish to speak with you today of your body weight and mind matters. You must both understand that your bodies are going through much more than the average person who is ascending into the fifth. You are ascending into much higher dimensions to be with us off and on for short periods of time. Not to worry. Your bodies will soon adapt to this and the weight should come off gradually. This was to be expected and we are terribly sorry for what you are going through...the feeling of being bloated, hard to breath, your minds not thinking clearly. We know of this and you both are being monitored at all times. Our galactic warriors, we send our love to you both at this time. We know the journey has been extremely hard and we are forever most proud of you and forever proud to be called your friends. Thank you for your time.

Thank you Federation

Sunday, September 21, 2008

Greetings, White Buffalo Calf Woman! Ashtar here with the Federation. Everything you are feeling, everything you are going through, is change. It is getting more difficult for you now to exist as so. We are counting the days as you are also. Do not expel too much energy worrying needlessly over small things. Take care of yourself; moment by moment, that's all that is required at this time. Happy days ahead, you'll see. Just ride out the storm for now. Blessings, dear one. The Federation thanks you for your time.

Thank you Ashtar and Federation

Monday, September 22, 2008

Greetings, White Buffalo Calf Woman! The Federation here wishing Daniel a very Happy Earth-Birth Day! Daniel, it has been fifty of your earth years since you came to the planet as Daniel Horn. It has been but a blink of an eye here on the starship. What a contrast! Time is a funny thing, is it not? To you both, the clock ticks ever nearer to our grand "coming out" party. So you see Daniel, one party right after another. Everything going according to plan for a world-wide celebration bar none. Think of us as much as we think of you and our grand reunion. Thank you for your time.

Thank You Federation

Tuesday, September 23, 2008

Greetings White Buffalo Calf Woman! The Federation here. Ah, the mystery of the crystals! Yes, you and Daniel know this is the reason we have asked for crystals to be placed outside. We see and we know. They will be most powerful. This will be a short communiqué as the closer the event date peaks over your horizon, the more chaotic your atmosphere will become. Know of this and take heed. All is well for a safe ascension. Thank you for your time.

Thank you Federation

Wednesday, September 24, 2008

Greetings White Buffalo Calf Woman! The Federation here. One of your earth days closer to reality. It has been quite a journey for eons of time… watching everyone on the earth plane "sleeping" their lives away. There were those who knew the truth but the vast majority really had no idea who they were. It has been quite the game. We are really extremely proud of all the souls who took part. Now, very slowly, they will awaken to the whole truth if they are willing to go that far. Thank you both for the last couple of years…it has been absolutely amazing watching both of you go from zero to one million in very little time. Your awakening has not been gradual like most and yet you both still manage, for the most part, to run your lives as normal human beings. To say we are proud does not even touch the emotions we are feeling at this time. Job extremely well done. Thank you for your time.

Thank you Federation

Thursday, September 25, 2008

Greetings White Buffalo Calf Woman! We, of the total of the Federation, wish to speak today. It was our mandate to tell the world of the date, October 14, 2008. At this time, we wish to give you the date October 4, 2008 as "First Contact". We wish to warn you of the extreme pandemonium that will occur, so please take heed and stay close to home quarters. If anything else of extreme importance should occur before this date, we will inform you. Thank you for your time.

Thank you Federation

Ho! You must listen to these words. They speak of truth. Be ready, be prepared. Your words of wisdom will be needed on this earth, our mother. Please come sit with us and pray for these times.

Thank you Guides

Friday, September 26, 2008

Greetings White Buffalo Calf Woman! The Federation High Council speaking. We have given you the date October 4 of this year…this is our intention at this time. We do not foresee any difficulties but if this time frame must be moved either forward or back, we will most certainly inform you. Our reason for giving you this date is that you will see we are directly talking to you and that you will fully believe it. We know it is most difficult to comprehend at times but this will be the proof. We wish this date to be kept between you, Daniel and the Federation at this time. This will be your way of showing others that you speak with us on a daily basis and are part of the Federation itself. Thank you for your time.

Thank you Federation

Saturday, September 27, 2008

Greetings White Buffalo Calf Woman! The Federation here. A lot of changes going on right now with your physical bodies…getting ready for your meetings with us or should we say "your return home"! Over the course of our entering into your atmosphere, we predict we will have to have more than one meeting as you will not be gone for long periods of time from your home base. You are needed there to quell the masses. Get yourselves mentally ready for the mass hysteria. This is why we must have many short meetings. All is well and in place for our descent. Thank Daniel for deciding to take the day before off. We will all need clear thinking minds. Yes, we know your minds are muddled. Nancy, you are so funny. Yes, we call you by your earth-given name through our communiqué…less writing for you. Keep well, both of you. See you very soon. Thank you for your time.

Thank you Federation

Monday, September 29, 2008

Greetings White Buffalo Calf Woman! This is the Federation speaking. We are ever closer now to our grand reunion. When we meet, you will return to your home with the tools and knowledge to put forth this great plan. It will be a busy time for you; maybe we can answer a few of your questions at this time. We wish to enter your atmosphere in the light morning hours of the 04. This way, the masses have many hours to see us and get used to our presence before the darkness of night descends upon the planet. We wish to give you some info on the mission at hand; yes, you will be given specifics but it will not take place right away, much for you and the crew who will be helping to get ready. Oh yes, your crew will be beamed aboard also, so they know their plans in the mission. This will avoid a lot of confusion after we leave as to who is doing what chores and how this will be planned. Of course, the "team" will have to have many meetings at your homes to figure out all the little details. Everyone will be so excited! Remember the importance of this…to educate the world! Of course, there will be other surprises involved; our little secret till we all meet. Till we see each other again. Thank you for your time.

Thank you Federation

Tuesday, September 30, 2008

Hello Nancy, our White Buffalo Calf Woman! The High Council, here once again, to speak of your galactic mission. At this time, we will not give all away as that would take away from our mission to you on the 04. We will tell you this, that you are correct in saying it will be a global mission. Of course, a lot of what you have spoken of is true, for your thoughts are divinely guided. There is also much more; the reason for your visit with us. As spoken in the communiqué yesterday, you will meet your "crew", some you know, others not. We here in the higher echelon, will be very happy to once again be face to face with our gentle warriors.

We really are so proud of you both. Thank you for your mission thus far; it has been quite a learning experience for all of us here on board. Thank you for your time.

Thank you High Council

Wednesday, October 1, 2008

Greetings White Buffalo Calf Woman! The Federation here. We have started our descent; all systems go. We are sorry for the ringing in your ears; it is because of our communication system between each other. As we descend and get closer to the planet, the ringing will probably persist. Try to ignore it. By the end of your week, you will probably be used to it and will not notice it as much. That is all for now. Thank you for your time.

Thank you Federation

Thursday, October 2, 2008

Greetings White Buffalo Calf Woman! The Federation here. We will not keep you long as we see you are tired. We wish to let it be known that we are very close now and you will be starting to really feel our presence. Your dogs feel it also. Over the next couple of days it will get very intense... not to worry at all. Remember, we are your friends and wish no harm to anyone on the planet. It will be due, of course, that some cannot handle our being in this atmosphere. It is those dear souls that agreed beforehand not to experience the ascension so that others may come. Try to keep this in mind...we know you are very soft hearted and wish too inform you of this ahead of time so that maybe the blow will not be so hard. We love you both dearly. Thank you for your time.

Thank you Federation

Friday, October 3, 2008

Greetings White Buffalo Calf Woman! The Federation here. Our descent is complete. Only the clicking of the clock stands between us now. Soon the guessing games will be over and the truth will be known. We are looking forward to a grand reunion like no other and the start of the next phase of our mission with earth. Remember to always tell others we come in peace with nothing but love in our hearts; for that is the biggest lesson of all. We are as anxious as you; always remember, though, to keep yourselves well grounded to mother earth at this time. That is all for now. Thank you for your time.

Thank you Federation

Saturday, October 4, 2008

Where are you? Why haven't you come? Morning hours?
Greetings White Buffalo Calf Woman! These things take time…the daylight has not gone. Keep a positive attitude and we will be there. Thank you for your time.

Thank you Federation

Sunday, October 5, 2008

Greetings White Buffalo Calf Woman! Ashtar here. This is so very hard to explain to you as you would not understand the concept I speak of. We had every intention of coming into your atmosphere yesterday but the conditions were not cohesive with our doing so. We understand our not showing up isn't validating your writings but you must go with what is in your heart. Do you believe or do you not? Did you see our ship or didn't you see our ship? Do you believe you traveled to your garden to see one of your native guides or didn't you? Remember your mental and physical being just after. Was that real? I think you know the answer to that. We will continue to try; you can continue to try from your end. Don't worry, we will soon meet; it is destiny. The whole key to this is to keep believing; know it in your heart to be true and it is. That is all for now. Blessings to you both.

Ashtar, are you still present to speak?

Yes, go ahead.

When will my veil be lifted?

Your veil will be lifted when we come into your atmosphere, which we hope is very soon. We just have to have the right doorway.

Shall I look for work in the meantime?

Looking for work, dear one, at this time, puts forth the vibration of "need". As you well know, if you are sending that, then that is what you receive back to you. What will your intent be?

Ashtar, so buying lottery tickets also puts out that "need" vibration?

Yes, thank you for asking that question. Just stop and see what happens, dear one.

Thank you Ashtar

Monday, October 6, 2008

Greetings White Buffalo Calf Woman! Ashtar here along with the High Council. We come today to give you our utmost sadness in that we could not appear this weekend. As we have seen from this weekend, it is not good to promise our sighting when circumstances make it otherwise. We truly are sorry for all your heartache. We will be there; you can count on that…it will be when it will be. It very well could be a spur of the moment happening. Yes, then your veils will be lifted and you will know your missions. Till then, relax and prepare. And so it is. Thank you for your time.

Thank you Ashtar and Federation High Council

Tuesday, October 7, 2008

Greetings White Buffalo Calf Woman! The Federation here. We are happy to say things are on schedule again; we will keep you posted. Once again, we are very sorry for last weekend not taking place as expected. Know in your heart we will be there. That is really all for now. Thank you for your time.

Thank you Federation

Ho! Yes, I am here. You wish me to speak to you. This is Broken Arm. I wish to speak of fear. Fear itself is not good; it makes you sick and shuts down your chakra system. This is why you become ill. Be happy; I am always here with you. I wish to talk more. You can ask me questions. I am your guide. I love you as you love me. Be strong. You are our warrior. I am proud. Thank you. Ho!

Thank you, Broken Arm

Wednesday, October 8, 2008

Greetings White Buffalo Calf Woman! Ashtar here with some very uplifting news. It is definitely a go for the fourteenth or before. We have run into a few quirks but everything is looking good. Keep looking to your skies and you will soon see us. Our little warriors, we await your visit with us. It will be a most uplifting experience for the two of you…one that you will be able to share with many others. Keep writing your book. Just keep the phrase "It will be a best seller" in your mind. You have both weathered the storm and will come out the better for it. Blessings to you both.

Thank you Ashtar

Thursday, October 9, 2008

Greetings White Buffalo Calf Woman! Ashtar here, once again. Everything will come to a head very soon. This chaotic world in which you live in,

I'm afraid, is going to get a little worse before it gets better. All in all, I think you know that in your heart; you feel the different energies in the atmosphere. As stated before, your mission will begin soon. You are going to rock the foundation of quite a few souls very worlds. Stay strong at heart, let your beliefs shine; don't listen to others who's vision and feelings don't match your own. This is the rule to live by; be yourself and you can't go wrong. Blessings, dear one, from all above.

Thank you Ashtar and to all above

Sunday, October, 12, 2008

Greetings White Buffalo Calf Woman! The Federation here with wishes of good tidings. Our meeting is only days away; we know you are as excited as we are. There are so many on your planet now that are walking the path of ascension. We are so pleased with the work all lightworkers have greatly contributed to this cause. It brings our hearts joy to see this massive turnaround. All lightworkers must realize it is not their fault the economy of the world and also the health of the earth is at an extreme all time low. This, of course, was to be; all part of the grand scheme of things. It was all part of the plan. Be joyous, be uplifted and most of all, as stated before, just be yourself. Keep shining love and light and we will meet again very, very soon. Many blessings to you on this day. Thank you for your time.

Thank you Federation

Monday, October 13, 2008

Greetings White Buffalo Calf Woman! Please get some rest as it will be a huge day tomorrow. We are in place and ready for our great descend. Hours now till our meeting. Blessings to you and Daniel. The Federation, signing off.

Thank you Federation

Tuesday, October 14, 2008

Greetings White Buffalo Calf Woman! The Federation here, Ashtar speaking. We are here; you do not need to give up on us. The time has not passed and we are still making ourselves known. Everything is still a big go. We feel every ones extreme energies; we know there are many who want us to show ourselves. With so many eagerly waiting friends, how could we not? Just try to keep yourself busy so to try and take your mind off of us for awhile. Tell Daniel we are still coming and of course your missions will still be a go. Thank you for waiting patiently for us…we certainly will not let you down. Thank you for speaking with me.

Thank you Ashtar and the Federation

Wednesday, October 15, 2008

Greetings White Buffalo Calf Woman! The High Council of the Federation here. We see such fear around you. Dear one, this is but a learning curve; both you and Daniel will be alright. You must understand that we are always looking out for your well being. You must understand the whole world is in chaos right now. You are not alone. We absolutely love you both dearly. Your life will once again come together. Do not mind about the dogs; they will adapt to your new life. You'll see, all will be well again. Yes, you both still have a mission. Unfortunately, we have had to abort this mission. Due to unforeseen circumstances, we were not able to enter the atmosphere. That is all we can say for now. We truly understand the pain you are in but you must remember that everything happens for a reason. Please stay in contact with us; it is always imperative that we not lose contact. Try to stay positive in these most difficult times, dear ones. With many blessings of love. Thank you for your time.

Thank You High Council

Thursday, October 16, 2008

Greetings White Buffalo Calf Woman! Ashtar here, once again, on behalf of the Federation. As I have said before, it was not for us to show up at this time due to the inactivation of a doorway. No, dear one, it had absolutely nothing to do with you or Daniel, as we know how much you were looking forward to our reunion. We have absolute faith that this will take place at some later date, when more of the masses are awakened. We are truly sorry for your heartache and I am diligently working behind the scenes for a special miracle for you both. This is all for now, my dear friends. Signing off with blessings from the Federation.

Thank you Ashtar and the Federation

Sunday, October 19, 2008

Greetings White Buffalo Calf Woman! We are here in place, awaiting your arrival. Go ahead.

Thank you. I ask to please speak to the High Council.

Yes Nancy, this is Ashtar speaking on behalf of the total of the High Council. I am addressing you as such as it is a shorter name than calling you by your true name, that which is White Buffalo Calf Woman.

Thank you Ashtar. My first question is...As I am White Buffalo Calf Woman, why is it I feel I am living in limbo, not knowing what to do or what direction to turn in?

Dear one, first off I wish to tell you that your life is never in limbo. What you do mean, I think, is why don't you know exactly what your mission is; therefore your life would flow in a certain direction. As stated before, your missions will be revealed when we can enter your atmosphere; which, I may add, really could be at any time. We are very sorry for this but there are galactic rules and regulations that must be followed.

This is not a blame game; you are not to blame us for our so called "no show" as we do not blame anyone on the earth plane for the uneventful moment in time. Please, I stress to you, go on as before, no fear, just live in the moment. Dear one, I am answering your questions as I speak so you do not have to go to the trouble of writing them again. Yes, you were nudged, so to speak, to keep all of our channeling's in a book form. As told before, we wish for you to tell your stories. You have the channeling's, you have started writing your life story as Nancy Simmons. This will then progress to the story of Nancy Horn and then to who you are today; our warrior, White Buffalo Calf Woman. You see, it is o.k. to feel lost at times, all part of your learning on the earth plane. Some days you feel strong, other days you feel small and frightened. The lesson is to have all your days feeling strong, tall and ready to tell the world who you are. When that happens, when you are believing and living your soul, the miracles start to happen. Now, I will enter upon the topic of the so called move. We know you are scared. Everything in existence has a timeline in which to stay or go. This too, is of your life in Port McNicoll…it's all energy. This may stay as so, it may not. Just as we had every intention of coming into the earth plane on the 14th, this did not happen. Do you not think that we too were not disappointed in this? We knew when this did not manifest, that there were thousands upon thousands of people very disappointed, even very mad at us. We do not like to see this from our brothers and sisters, as you must remember, we know you and this hurts us greatly. That is all I wish to say for now as per your home. As per prior events, we will not promise anymore. Just keep positive and hope for the best. You have also asked us who Daniel is. Yes, Daniel and you are together for a reason. He really needs to step up to the heart centre and do some connecting. He will find his answers. He hears us and should be channeling also. Dear one, as for feeling spiritually disconnected, that is only you doing so. You are going through a difficult time right now and need to try and stay centered as much as possible. We love you both so and wish you to know we are not "punishing" you for anything. Just know that things are as they should be and please keep in daily contact with us. Please don't forget to pray. Blessings to you both. Thank you for your time.

Thank you Ashtar and Council

Wednesday, October 22, 2008

Greetings White Buffalo Calf Woman! Ashtar here. We, of the Federation, are so happy to see you have begun to work through your fears. Your beautiful bright light is once again beginning to shine through. We know some lessons are tougher than others but please believe me when I say you shall pass through this into a wonderful new tomorrow. New places, new opportunities; this was but a moment in time. Do you know what kind of beautiful energy you will leave behind in that home for the next family? And on the story unfolds. We know your heart yearns for your mission to start; but all in the perfect moment. We have lots of those and you will see that White Buffalo Calf Woman will too. Please, I must stress to you, that although we know at this time you are busy with packing, etc., we also want you to keep at your writing. You see, the book is important. It will be heartfelt and something everyone will want to read. My little warrior, chin up, keep moving forward into your destiny for you will become one of the greatest teachers of all time. Blessings, dear one.

Thank you Ashtar

Sunday, October 26, 2008

Greetings White Buffalo Calf Woman! This is the High Council of the Galactic Federation speaking. We come to you this day for your confirmation, which, at this time, you so greatly need. You see, it is a universal law that the old must leave to make room for the new. This is what is presently happening in your reality. We understand your attachment to your surroundings but you see, dear one, this must go. It really has boiled down to too much upkeep and not enough time for spiritual matters; matters of the heart. So you see, even though your heart grieves now, in the end you will be a much stronger person for it. I know, as well as the rest of the council, you greatly wish and hope for our reunion soon. We understand you wish to begin your missions but all in due time. Something that has been planned for eons of time cannot and will not be broken. Take care, dear one. Look after yourself. This is Inus speaking on behalf of the High Council of the Galactic Federation. Thank you for your time.

Thank you Inus and High Council

Wednesday, October 29, 2008

May I ask a few questions?

Greetings White Buffalo Calf Woman! This is, once again, the High Council of the Galactic Federation speaking. Ashtar here. Go ahead, you may ask any questions you may have. I am, at this time, sitting with the High Council and we wish to answer any and all questions you may have.

I may have asked this question before, but do both Dan and I belong to the Ashtar Command, or should I say, are we members of the Ashtar Command?

The answer to that question is a definite yes! You can both be secure in the knowledge that you are both beloved members of the Ashtar Command. We have different divisions, each making up the totality of the command. As you both probably know, you fall under Archangel, or as we refer to him here, Lord Michael's Legion. You are both extremely revered and loved for the work you are doing.

I realize there is a timeline, so to say, for everything to happen; for things to fall into place. As light workers, we both are honored; I'm sure I speak for Dan also, to be given such an important duty. Speaking from my heart, I hope one day to see a great majority of the masses (I'm hoping for everyone!!!) to become enlightened. Both Dan and I feel there is something else we are to be doing (possibly teaching)? I have felt this would be on a very large scale…going out to the masses. Is this true…a huge mission that we will be part of?

Your feelings are always your truth. I would have to say the ascension is, in itself, a big deal. You are both very loving and compassionate light workers and although you may not see it on a day to day basis, have affected quite a few others with your love and light. This being said, yes, you both are two of the many from the home base, who have other missions that will take place when the time is right. Do not worry about when this will happen;

just be secure in the knowledge that it will take place. As I have stated, before, follow your heart, it will never lie to you.

Ashtar, is there anything else you would like to say at this time?

You are both in a transitory state right now. Everything in your life seems to be in upheaval; you are both "unwell" now, mentally and physically. You shall pass through this phase into a "new easier life", shall we say. One that is not so chaotic. All part of your missions as Lord Michael's Legion members and therefore, of course, important members of the Ashtar Command. Dear ones, hold steadfast, look to a bright new tomorrow and know in your hearts, everything is well and as it should be. We thank you, brave ones, for everything you are going through and for walking forward with heads held high. Our mighty warriors! Blessings to you both, and from the High Council, thank you for your time.

Thank you Ashtar and High Council

Friday, October 31, 2008

Greetings White Buffalo Calf Woman! You see, you are integrating quite nicely into the apartment building. This is Ashtar speaking of the Galactic Federation Ashtar Command. I am reiterating that fact as you are in a difficult environment at this time. Once things settle down and you get yourself into a routine once again, you'll see that things will change for the better. We had promised, quite awhile ago, that we would bring people to you and we will. This will eventually bring you out to your mission; out to the masses, should we say. This all takes time but things worth waiting for usually do. Walk forward, head held high like the true goddess you are; our goddess of the buffalo. We shall speak soon. Blessings to you both.

Thank you Ashtar

Sunday, November 2, 2008

Greetings White Buffalo Calf Woman! Ashtar here. I am so pleased to speak with you today. We, of the higher realms, realize the enormous amount of pain you are experiencing at this time. We do understand, that is the reason we have not spoken with you on a daily basis. We truly miss our daily communication and hope that once this "instance" is over and done with, that we may resume our daily talks. I do not mean to seem cold-hearted when I say "instance", for I know in your linear time, it is much more than an "instance". I do speak in terms of our time here. You shall come through this and be more stronger for it. Just always remember your mission. This is all leading up to a greatness you cannot imagine. Keep yourself healthy, dear one. Blessings to you both.

Thank you Ashtar

Monday, November 3, 2008

Greetings White Buffalo Calf Woman! It is I, Ashtar and the High Council of the Galactic Federation of Light. We see you are unwell; please, dear one, you must remember to smudge yourself everyday and do your infinity breath. This is extremely important for you and for everyone around you. We know these are difficult times; please pace yourself, everything will be done in time. Keep well, dear one. You are most beloved. Blessings to you both and thank you for your time.

Thank you Ashtar and High Council

Tuesday, November 4, 2008

Greetings White Buffalo Calf Woman! Ashtar here. It is good to see the change in your aura just by smudging yourself and surrounding yourself in light. You must get back into the routine of doing this on a daily basis. It is important for your well being. Both you and Daniel will be very busy, so keep yourself in good health. Blessings to you both.

Thank you Ashtar

Sunday, November 9, 2008

Greetings White Buffalo Calf Woman! Ashtar here. The move is complete and now you can take time settling in. Remember, Rome wasn't built in a day. I know at this time you would rather be in Port McNicoll, but you will soon have evidence that where you are now is exactly the place you should be. Remember, it's not always what it seems. Look ahead to much brighter, future days. You have come through this quite well, our little warrior. You have had communication with another as of late; all o.k., from the Flagship Nibiru. Others shall speak with you also. You are their lady, White Buffalo Calf Woman. Don't be surprised when you go online, if you have the urge, more and more, to have dialogue with others. It is time. As stated before, changes will be happening quickly; you are now getting through the worst. It should be a wonderful glide for you now. Blessings to you both.

Thank you Ashtar

Thursday, November 13, 2008

Greetings White Buffalo Calf Woman! Ashtar here. We have come to see this move is not going very well for you. We see your heart is broken and you really do not want to unpack. We, of the Federation, did not know it would be this hard of an adjustment for you. You see, dear one, every situation can go one way or another. We had hoped for a much better outcome as we thought living in an apartment would be easier on both of you. There would, of course, be a few minor adjustments; walking the dogs being one and living in a smaller space being another. Of course, the hardest would be living in a city again. Now we fear you will not be able to go forward with your mission at this residence. We fear we have maybe made a mistake in sending you here. We know you can handle the mission; we wanted to hear you say it. As stated before, dear one, you have been sent here as this is where your "peeps", as you would call them, are situated. Please look forward to a better future; you don't have to stay here forever, remember. When you start your mission, you can move back up north, if that is what you want. We know you miss the area, but maybe only for a short while. We send blessings and roses your way hoping it will make your day a little nicer. Blessings to you both.

Thank you Ashtar

Thursday, November 20. 2008

Greetings White Buffalo Calf Woman! Ashtar here. As we, of the Federation, sit and watch, we wonder at the possibilities that sit in your realm. You are so close right now, so close you can almost reach out and touch success. Will it happen? Without a doubt, for the arena has been cleared for positive reinforcement. All is in place, ready to go. Just stay in the moment and relax. All is on schedule. You will see everything come together. All for a happy reunion. Blessings to you both.

Thank you Ashtar

Monday, November 24, 2008

Greetings White Buffalo Calf Woman! Ashtar here with greetings of thankfulness and of coming home again. We, of the Federation, are extremely happy to see once again, you settling into a routine of communication and of meditation. It is a wondrous day, is it not? We understand there has been much transition in your life as late but we assure you the worst is over. Now, the next step is the step to healthfulness. We are extremely proud of the weight loss and the over all picture of looking after oneself. We know you can do this and when needed, a little prod from your friends of above. Blessings, dear one.

Thank you Ashtar

Tuesday, November 25, 2008

Greetings White Buffalo Calf Woman! We, the High Council of the Federation, wish to speak with you this day. It is of utmost importance that we see you through this mission. You have previously asked for our help and we have involved ourselves within your mission. We must say at this time, you are where you should be. Place, time, energy mean everything. We tell you that 2009 will be a very important year. Stay in the moment with no worries as you are always guided by those above at critical junctures. Know this, for it is important for your well being. Blessings and thank you for your time.

Thank you High Council

Friday, November 28, 2008

Thank you everyone for the Gift!

Greetings White Buffalo Calf Woman! Ashtar here with the High Council. We wish to say "You are very welcome". You have been so traumatized lately that this is our way of giving back and in hopes that you will stay strong. You have been speaking lately with the Nibiru High Council and others aboard the ship. There are many councils on board and they will tell you if they are from the light. If you ask, they must always tell the truth. So, knowing this, of course, it is alright to speak with them. They are your warriors, so to speak, and will always look after your well being, as you can see from your phone conversation this morning. We will say that we are most proud that you stepped forward and made the call, knowing it was a hard move for you to make. One more step forward. You see, dear one, you will persevere through any situation that arises through your life on the earth plane. That is all we wish to speak of today. Blessings, dear one.

Thank you Ashtar and High Council

Sunday, November 30, 2008

Greetings White Buffalo Calf Woman! Ashtar here. We, of the Galactic Federation, understand that you are noticing distinct global changes within your world. We will tell you that it must get worse before everyone understands what is taking place. We are pleased to say, however, it will not be as bad as was speculated. The light has traveled and grown so fast; more than we had anticipated. And for that, we are eternally grateful to all of our light workers. All have exceeded our expectations. As stated before, troubled times still lay ahead. All, ground work for the most amazing, eventful times on earth. The cleansing must take place to make room for enormous changes. This, dear one, is taking place now in your own personal space. You are following our gentle nudges and we are so grateful for this also. Our warrior is on her way. Blessings, dear one.

Thank you Ashtar

Wednesday, December 3, 2008

Greetings White Buffalo Calf Woman! The Federation of Light here; we are the High Council. Your spokesperson today is Irahol. Yes, I have spoken before; I am from the starship Nibiru. We are one and the same. I am very pleased to be able to speak with you this day. Our line of communication is opening up splendidly. We hear your thoughts and wish to speak today of something that has been on your mind for quite some time now. We wish to speak of who you are and also of your mission. You ARE ABSOLUTELY who you say you are; you feel it in your heart but you just can't seem to come to terms with that in your mind. Your ego is doing quite a bit of kicking and screaming, is it not? We tell you to just keep on doing what you are doing. Soon, all will be revealed and you will understand your place in the big picture. This also goes for your mission. Very soon, you will know your teachings and what to do. As stated some time before, people will come to you and you will know, without a shadow of a doubt, that they are to work with you. No worries; relax in the perfect moment of now. We are so glad to see you having a perfect moment last night. You did enjoy yourself. Thank you for your time.

Thank you Irahol and High Council

Thursday, December 4, 2008

Greetings White Buffalo Calf Woman! Ashtar here with greetings from myself and the Command. We wish today to speak of first contact, which will be happening early in the new year. You will be prepared ahead of time for your mission and for our return. It is time for everyone to become aware of the changing of power upon the earth. So many live their day to day lives not knowing what is going on in the big picture. We know you are anxiously awaiting your mission to move forward and speak your truth. Soon, very soon we say, for the ones in power are crumbling with no way to save themselves. Blessings to you.

Thank you Ashtar and Command

Friday, December, 5, 2008

Greetings White Buffalo Calf Woman! Speaking from the Nibirian High Council, Jachino here. Your Ashtar is present here also. You wish me to speak today of your drum. You see, it is there sitting to the side, and you are not able to be with her. It frustrates you, does it not? There is a time for everything; everything is perfect in the moment, so there is naught to be frustrated about. You must put a little more effort into your weight loss; we are so pleased to see it has come down. Keep trying; there are many energetic days ahead of you. All is according to plan. Thank you for your time.

Thank you Jachino, High Council and Ashtar

Tuesday, December 9, 2008

Greetings White Buffalo Calf Woman! Ashtar here with greetings of abundance. You will very soon see an upward spiral in your financial situation. Everything is coming together. The players will unfold and the story of the millennia will come forth into fruition.

You are doing exactly what you should be at this time. Blessings to you both, dear one.

Thank you Ashtar

Thursday, December 11, 2008

Greetings White Buffalo Calf Woman! Ashtar and the Command present today. We, as a collective, would like to illustrate to you today, the importance of being true to oneself. It is imperative at this time, you follow the teachings of your heart. We see you are very confused right now and wish to add that we would never put you into a situation that would cause you harm or cause you to give up on your mission. This has come too far for it all to be thrown away at this time. Does that answer your questions, dear one? Everyday can be as perfect as you make it. For it is in this perfect moment that one can be true to the self. Always remember this as you step forward to your mission and a bright, new future for tomorrow. Blessings to you both, dear one.

Thank you Ashtar and Command

Sunday, December 14, 2008

Greetings White Buffalo Calf Woman. Ashtar here. We, of the Federation, wish to answer a few things you have been pondering lately within your soul. Yes, yes and yes! These are the answers to your questions. As we have stated before, you always discern right from wrong. You do not have to second guess yourself. You are of Federation status, therefore treat your knowledge as such. Yes, huge changes are ahead; all for the betterment of yourself and others around you. You also have a big part to play in the ascension process. All will be revealed soon. Blessings to you, dear one.

Thank you Ashtar

Saturday, December 20, 2008

Greetings White Buffalo Calf Woman! Ashtar here. We are glad to have you back within the fold. You see, to discern your true feelings is of the utmost importance. Soon, my friend, we will walk forward in a peaceful way; helping others to act in accordance. Peace and harmony will reign as superior on earth. Isn't it what was planned all along? For the light is shining so brightly from so many hearts. You see what is happening now in front of you. The dark must soon step down from their place of power. When this takes place, I promise you, we will be there in a flash, to assist. Such exciting times ahead. All will look about them in wonder. Most will be in shock at how they were deceived by so many, for so long. It will take time to recover the trust of the masses, but this too shall take place. Rest up, dear one, for the road ahead will be fraught with sleepless nights and exciting new days. Blessings to you both.

Thank you Ashtar

Wednesday, December 24, 2008

Greetings, dear one! The Federation, once again, with wishes for a wonderful holiday full of peace. Once again, it is a time for families to come together and reconnect. We wish to see the light and love that is shining this time of year, to be shining the whole year through. We know it is your fondest wish also. Take some time for yourself to reconnect with yourself, for you do not have to run to the aid of all. Remember. We shall be happy to connect with you on a more regular basis. Happy Holidays! Thank you for your time.

Thank you Federation

Friday, December 26, 2008

Greetings White Buffalo Calf Woman! Ashtar here with greetings from family and friends. I wish to speak today of harmony. You have been able to see and feel harmony in many aspects of your life. There have been times when much has been felt and other times when it seems to be missing. These are the times that teach us the greatest lessons. It is the day to day trivial opportunities that one often misses when not in harmony with all. There is not a soul on earth that has not missed many of these, for often the eyes as well as the mind is often closed to them. Always be focused on the now so that you operate on balance and harmony; two keys that are extremely important on one's journey through the ascension. Dear one, when it is your time to step forward with your mission, it is essential you be operating from both. Once again, know we are looking forward to reuniting with you once again. Blessings.

Thank you Ashtar

Saturday, December 27, 2008

Greetings White Buffalo Calf Woman! Ashtar here. We, the Federation are happy to see you settling into a routine once again. We know it is difficult; just remember that miracles do and will happen. So much momentum to move forward once again, as you have many hopes and dreams, all within your reach. Sometimes it seems we must step backward to move forward again. Sometimes a lesson must be learned to begin anew; to step onto ones chosen path. These things happen and although it does not make much sense at the time, the truth of the instance becomes apparent later on. Stay centered, stay true to yourself. Live your truth. Blessings to you, dear one.

Thank you Ashtar

Sunday, December 28, 2008

Greetings White Buffalo Calf Woman! Ashtar here with the Federation in its entirety. We must be together in earnest as the days are passing. You will soon have the veil lifted and your mission will begin in earnest with those you are to work side by side with. We will be in constant contact; please, when you hear a loud ringing within your ears, please stop what you are doing and come to us. It is getting to the point where I cannot stress this enough. Thank you for waiting through thick and thin; we know it hasn't been easy. Much love and many blessings to you, dear one!

Thank you Ashtar and Federation

Monday, December 29, 2008

Greetings White Buffalo Calf Woman! Ashtar here, on behalf of the Federation, my Command and Lord Michaels Legions. We are stepping up to the days of the great awakening for all those who where sent to the earth plane as divine teachers. Those who have important missions in the days to come, will feel a distinct change within themselves. Their beings are changing at a rapid pace which you see evidence of already. These are exciting times ahead; we feel the excitement around us and feel the love glowing from those, our brave teachers, our brave friends. We are in awe of that which has taken place at such an alarming rate on the earth plane, and still our "missionaries" , shall we call you, still stand tall, shining outwards for all to see. We cannot thank you enough for what you have accomplished thus far. We know, without a doubt, that our grand mission to see earth and her inhabitants ascend to the next level of consciousness, is a grand success. Thank you one and all. Blessings to you, dear one.

Thank you Ashtar, Federation, Command and Legion

Tuesday, December 30, 2008

Greetings White Buffalo Calf Woman! Ashtar here. Greetings to you on this day; almost at years end. Take some time today and tomorrow, to reflect over the past year and then let the many hardships go; ready to begin a new fresh year. 2009 promises to be better in so many ways. We hope you are preparing yourself for the many challenges ahead. All good. We are on constant watch, sometimes with much glee and laughter. If anything, sometimes we have to step back and have a good laugh, right

Daniel? "This is your captain speaking". I never thought just one sentence could make you jump in fear and hang up the phone. One of these days, Daniel, one of these days! Are we a little nervous? No need to be that way; we are old friends. No need for fear from either of you; you are both extremely loved and adored by family and friends alike. Many blessings on this quite amusing day.

Thank you Ashtar

YEAR
2009

Friday, January 9, 2009

Good morning, White Buffalo Calf Woman! Ashtar here. Greetings for a very prosperous New Year! This is the first day of the new year that we have been able to communicate properly; on the ninth day, of the first month in the year 2009. It is very good indeed.; your beginning, into who you will project out into the world. This is the year of standing up for yourself. No one will make your decisions for you; you, and only you, will decide what is best for you. This will take some getting used to but will be what is needed in the end. We see you are indeed making sure the body and spirit are being rid of all toxicity. Keep yourself within the purist of light so that you may heal. We are looking forward to the year ahead with much anticipation for all that is to be. Blessings to you, dear one.

Thank you Ashtar

White Buffalo Calf Woman! This is Arcturus here. I am from the starship Nibiru and would like to clarify that our ship was spotlighted in your earthly skies. We will have a constant contact with you soon. It is time to progress to the next level of your advancement. I wish to clarify that you will have nightly visits from us until such time that that you understand your mission. Yes, I am from the light and am looking forward to meeting you soon. Thank you for your time.

Thank you Arcturus

Saturday, January 10, 2009

Greetings White Buffalo Calf Woman! Ashtar here. Thank you for taking better care of yourself, your earthly body. Please look at this as a new start, to a new person, in a new year. Just know we are with you on your mission every step of the way. Never doubt this. Many changes taking place in your life to make way for the new. Always remember your people. We promise things will start rolling soon as far as your mission is concerned. Do not worry about what or who you cannot change; that is not for you to be concerned about. Look after yourself now, dear one. Blessings to you.

Thank you Ashtar

Sunday, January 11, 2009

Greetings White Buffalo Calf Woman! Ashtar here on behalf of the rest of the Federation. We are so lucky to be able to be in contact with you one on one. There are others who are to begin their missions, who, for one reason or another, cannot communicate with us. Your time is ever drawing nearer; just keep positive and all will go according to plan. These will be exciting times for you. We understand your frustration at not knowing or understanding what is going on, but there, of course, is a reason for that. Just know that it will happen soon. There are many who will cheer you on, little warrior. Blessings to you.

Thank you Ashtar and Federation

Monday, January 12, 2009

The first day back to work for Dan, after the holidays, and already I feel I'm being bombarded by negative energy from the family. Please, someone, how can I fix this? I feel whenever I'm around any of them, even over the phone, negative energy!!!???

Ho! Greetings White Buffalo Calf Woman! This is Seven Hawks speaking. I am one of your guides and am here to speak with you. I see you worry about your father and your mother and that is o.k. When our parents become elders and they are not well or are not of sound mind, it is our nature to be concerned; to protect those who once protected us. The rest of your siblings seem to want to do this also but with very much drama involved. It is not in your best interest to get involved in all the drama. You must put "you" first at this time. It does not mean you are not concerned for your mother and father; you have to step back and let the rest of them continue on with their scenario. There will be times when you can see your father and mother without the fanfare. I really feel for you when the negativity is bombarding you from all sides. Stay strong, our warrior; stay on course and see your teaching through to the end. It will start soon, I promise you. Ho!

Thank you Seven Hawks

Tuesday, January 13, 2009

Greetings White Buffalo Calf Woman! Ashtar here. We, the Federation are always here to help, along with your guides and angels. The end of all conflict is fast approaching your world, in which time, all will be revealed to both you and Daniel. We know, on your timeline, it has been a very long wait, but has been no longer than the blink of an eye to us. We understand that things cannot move forward as it stands now. Please, dear one, be patient for just awhile longer. We know you hunger for peace in all areas of your life and for the lives of all others. This will be so. Part of the reason for so much turmoil at this time is that the energy around and on Mother Earth is changing at a rapid pace. Just stay positive and know that big changes, big positive changes are coming your way. Blessings to you, dear one.

Thank you Ashtar and Federation

Wednesday, January 14, 2009

Greetings White Buffalo Calf Woman! Ashtar, with news from above and beyond. All systems are go for a quick and successful first contact with those we need to speak with. We, dear one, will soon set the ball rolling on a course to peace, love and prosperity for all. Your teachings will begin in earnest very soon. Thank you for being ever faithful and sticking to your own beliefs, no matter what those around may think. Blessings to you, dear one.

Thank you Ashtar

Friday, January 16, 2009

Greetings White Buffalo Calf Woman! Such a laugh we have just had. Writing is clearly over-rated, but I know you wish to keep your messages; so it is what it is. This is Ashtar speaking on behalf of the Command and the Federation. We are, at this time, sitting in council, going over our objectives, with you in our minds eye at all times. We know you are as excited as we are at this time to "get the ball rolling" shall we say. Soon, very soon, is all we can say at this time. The date for our great reunion is etched in time. Look forward with great enthusiasm to the very time of which we speak. Again, thank you for your patience and blessings to you, dear one.

Thank you Ashtar, the Command and the Federation

Sunday, January 18, 2009

Greetings White Buffalo Calf Woman! I am Seven Hawks and wish to speak with you today. You seem very frustrated. You do not know where to turn. This is a difficult time for you. It is hard, backing away from the family. Duality runs rampant within your family. Some days, things are good, other days, everyone gets on your nerves. How can you move forward when you are stuck? You must make a decision; being told what to do, or make your own decisions for yourself? Once you make a decision, do not feel guilty, for what you decide is best for you. That is all. To make your decisions and not have someone else make them for you. You will do what you have to do, when you have to do it. I am your guide and happy to speak with you. I am happy you can hear me and feel my presence. This is good. All of your guides love you dearly. Ask questions and we will answer. Love and light to you. Ho!

Thank you Seven Hawks

Monday, January 19, 2009

Greetings White Buffalo Calf Woman! Ashtar here on behalf of the Federation. We have come to a time where it is safe to move forward in our ventures. You will soon see evidence of much more communication between us. Listen to your ears ringing, see evidence of the "white feather", it all means the same, please come sit and talk with us. The time for planning our great reunion is soon and it is time for our ground crew to be ready. It will soon be time to speak with your people, those who are getting the same messages as you are. Stay positive. Blessings to you, dear one.

Thank you Ashtar and Federation

Good afternoon! I'm a little slow on the draw! Greetings, dear one. This is Ashtar; glad to see you have noticed the sign. And so it is. We will communicate. Blessings to you, dear one.

Thank you Ashtar

Tuesday, January 20, 2009

Greetings White Buffalo Calf woman! Ashtar here and history has been made. Time for the ground crew to get down to business, shall we say. It is my great honour to welcome all of you back into the fold. It has been awhile, some would say too long. Many eons have passed, a lot of struggles and now you can look forward to a brighter future. Another of our dark players has left the stage. I too, wish to say, "Job well done". Let the party begin! Blessings to you, dear one.

Thank you Ashtar

Wednesday, January 21, 2009

Greetings White Buffalo Calf Woman! Ashtar here. We now start a new phase on earth; a new phase that will usher in peace and abundance for all on earth. It is a time of reckoning for those who fall within the dark legions, for their actions will be called forth and dealt with. Yes, they will be given the utmost respect and will deal with what has transpired on their own. Our time is quickly being called forth, and with that, we are greatly looking forward. You will hear of this over your news waves, over the next few weeks. And so it is. Blessings to you, dear one.

Thank you Ashtar

Friday, January 23, 2009

Greetings White Buffalo Calf Woman! Ashtar here along with the Command and members of the Federation. We are present at this time to speak on the days and weeks ahead for you and for planet Earth. Very shortly, you will see signs of our "working behind the scenes" in your favor. We have moved the date, of your coming out, forward, to progress with what is happening on earth at this time. We must keep everyone moving in a forward motion. Do not be alarmed by your so called illness; you are being raised up energetically by light at a rapid pace. Be still; have moments of quietness. This feeling will pass as your body adjusts. This must take place to move on with your mission and to completely understand that which must be done. This will require a clear mind in which to teach, for teach you will. The Federation will be present, so in the coming weeks, must be a first contact of sorts. Keep looking to the skies, dear one, for soon you shall see evidence of what we speak is the truth. Many blessings to you, dear one.

Thank you Ashtar, Command and Federation

Sunday, January 25, 2009

Greetings White Buffalo Calf Woman! Ashtar here, once again, with the Command and members of the Federation. We spoke to you of what will transpire over the next few weeks and so it shall. These times call for more joyous moments than what was previously known in the past. We are not only working on the light body at this time, but are also working on others which will be in your group of teachers. To get the ball rolling, shall we say, others must awaken to their purpose and their reasons for being around you. This is what we work on at this time while other more worldly scenarios play out and enter the space of light and love. We will keep you briefed as to what is transpiring. Blessings to you, dear one.

Thank you Ashtar, Command and Federation

Monday, January 26, 2009

Greetings White Buffalo Calf Woman! Ashtar here. The days are progressively moving forward and all work undertaken by us is underway. There is still work to be done and much planning as to when we can finally be in constant contact with our earth warriors. This will be a short communiqué this day. All is still on board. Blessings, dear one.

Thank you Ashtar

Thursday, January 29, 2009

Greetings White Buffalo Calf Woman! Ashtar here with wonderful news. The date for first contact moves ever forward with each passing day. The enlistment of many dear souls on your earth grows; grows more and more each day. We sometimes have to sit back and look with much wonderment at what is happening. I ask you to please keep positive, as this is what you need to be doing at this time. Blessings to you, dear one.

Thank you Ashtar

Sunday, February 1, 2009

Greetings White Buffalo Calf Woman! Ashtar here. The time is close at hand when we will be reunited together; all of the ground crew with your space brothers and sisters. As glorious as it will be, we have some serious business to attend to. It is time to wake up the rest of humanity. Thank you for listening to me this morning; I must speak to you whenever the time is available. Blessings to you, dear one.

Thank you Ashtar

Monday, February 2, 2009

Greetings White Buffalo Calf Woman! Ashtar here with Aukmuk. You have both spoken in earnest before. Aukmuk is guiding you along your way as are the rest of us whom you speak with. All will come out soon. There is still much for you to take in, so rest is needed. It will surely not be long now. Blessings, dear one.

Thank you Ashtar and Aukmuk

Tuesday, February 3, 2009

Greetings White Buffalo Calf Woman! Ashtar here. The time is very soon now, dear one. Those of you will slowly start to come together for the sake of all mankind. It starts this week and will continue on till all are present. Thank you, dear one, for your patience. We know it has been difficult to keep up the positive front for so long. Blessings to you, dear one.

Thank you Ashtar

Wednesday, February 4, 2009

Greetings White Buffalo Calf Woman! Ashtar here. The days of our reunion are ever closer. We need to start our planning very soon as time moves ever forward. Sananda says to keep moving forward with your exercises; he promises you will see great changes shortly. We forever admire you for the struggles you have been through, for it has made you into a great leader that you will soon be for a great number of others. Blessings to you, dear one.

Thank you Ashtar and Sananda

Thursday, February 5, 2009

Greetings White Buffalo Calf Woman! Ashtar here. I promise you it will not be long now. Even as we speak, everything is coming together quite nicely. You may have much to talk about tomorrow; it will all come together. It is time to start collecting the ground crew for there is much to get together. Much planning. Blessings to you, dear one.

Thank you Ashtar

Friday, February 6, 2009

Greetings White Buffalo Calf Woman! Ashtar here. I wish to speak today of chances. Today is a good day for many. Any time you may see one, ask for its manifestation. Remember, there are many around you who would love to help. Many guides, angelic beings, light beings and yes, of course, the Federation, are always watching and waiting. Be diligent but let the conversations flow where they will go. Never force the issue; that is a general rule that we adhere to. If questions are asked, answer to the best of your ability. I, personally, will be around for guidance. Blessings to you, dear one.

Thank you Ashtar

Saturday, February 7, 2009

Well, greetings White Buffalo Calf Woman! Sananda speaking. We are still waiting for you to claim your heritage. You cannot go forward until you have done so. Keep searching and you will find what it is you need to know. This is important and should not be taken lightly. Thank you, dear soul, for your time.

Thank you Sananda

Monday, February 9, 2009

Greetings White Buffalo Calf Woman! Ashtar here, once again, with Sananda. We wish to speak today of gaining much of your energy back. You must realize, when you go outside, there is much around that bask in your light. After awhile, it gets very depleted. You must drink plenty of water and eat lightly, for this is what the body needs at this time. Remember to always replenish your soul by remembering who you are. Live it, breathe it, know it. Your mission is fast approaching and we want you to be more than ready, dear one. We see your light, dear one. Let it shine for everyone. Blessings to you, dear one.

Thank you Sananda and Ashtar

Tuesday, February 10, 2009

Greetings White Buffalo Calf Woman! Ashtar here with Sananda and Lord Michael of the Legions. We see so much of your spirit shining through now. All things seem to be coming at you now. These are tests, nothing else. Just keep riding the waves of light as you have been doing. We are pleased with the progress you are making in general. Just keep thinking your beautiful thoughts. Know who you are. Live it, breathe it, know it. All is well and on track. Blessings to you, dear one.

Thank you Ashtar, Sananda and Lord Michael

Good evening, White Buffalo Calf Woman! Sananda speaking, wishing you the best. It is the beginning of the lessons you will learn in order to move forward; lessons you already know but have long forgotten. This will be done in a way as not to alarm you. Welcome us into your heart as we welcome you back into the fold. Thank you and blessings.

Thank you Sananda

Wednesday, February 11, 2009

Greetings White Buffalo Calf Woman! Ashtar here, once again, with Sananda. Keep up the exuberance of life and all that is shortly going to be taking place. We still see some hesitation about matters at hand. Once again, we will repeat to you, just go with what feels right to your heart. Don't flip flop back and forth. You know you are protected at all times.

One minute I feel I shouldn't do something and the next I feel it is my duty to help others along the path.

Once again, we both say, "What is your heart truly telling you"?

It certainly was not giving off bad vibes. So, I will do what I think is right.

That is all we ever ask of you; to do what is right for you. We say to you, use your protection wherever you go. That is all. Thank you for your time and blessings to you.

Thank you Sananda and Ashtar

Thursday, February 12, 2009

Greetings White Buffalo Calf Woman! Ashtar here, with Sananda, once again. Dear lady, we can see and feel your urge to teach but it is not quite time for that manifestation. It will be quite an experience for you and for all others. Keep it burning in your heart. We know it has been there for some time. Everything is still on target as far as First Contact Mission is concerned. We are making great headway with this situation. Stay focused in the moment, dear one, and keep the heart fires burning. Blessings to you always.

Thank you Ashtar and Sananda

Good afternoon, White Buffalo Calf Woman! This is the Spiritual Hierarchy of Nine. We welcome you to this journey of the senses and of the mind. There are so many places to go within a dimension; to see, to hear, to feel. We tell you to be ever more observant of everything and everyone around you, for you will see others. That is all. Thank you for your time.

Thank you Spiritual Hierarchy of Nine

Friday, February 13, 2009

Greetings White Buffalo Calf Woman! Ashtar and Sananda here, once again. We wish to tell our goddess to make the most out of this day. It is magic in the making, is it not? We are so excited to see every step forward that is taken, be it ever so slightly. These are the times things will take a turn for the betterment of all, be it earthly or universally. We ask you, from our heart to yours, have a grand day and make the most out of every single minute. Blessings to you, dear one.

Thank you Ashtar and Sananda

Saturday, February 14, 2009

Greetings White Buffalo Calf Woman! Ashtar speaking. I wish to address the topic of family. Dear one, you dwell on so many topics inside your mind, is it any wonder that it is very hard for you to concentrate. There are reasons and you know why the family circle seems to be falling away. It is to be so. Everyone has a path; a journey they must undertake. Please, let them go on the journey. Let them go. Let them be. You have more important issues at hand. Number one should be your own journey. Stay focused. Stay true to yourself. Never apologize for what you must do in the moment. Let your heart speak. It will always tell you the truth. Friends are now falling away to make way for the new. You see and sense this also.

Let it all happen. You will soon see evidence of the magic happening all around you. Stay focused, dear one. Many blessings to you.

Thank you Ashtar

Sunday, February 15, 2009

Greetings White Buffalo Calf Woman! Ashtar here. You will start to feel an exhilaration of energy very soon. I feel you have started; a little bit of dizziness. As stated before, things will be happening now at a rapid pace. It is all starting to fall into place. Stay focused. Blessings to you, dear one.

Thank you Ashtar

Tuesday, February 17, 2009

Greetings White Buffalo Calf Woman! Ashtar here with Sananda and Michael. We wish to discuss energy today. Energy affects people in different ways. The more enlightened one is, the more that soul will be able to positively handle the heightened energies that are coming to earth at this time. Some will not be able to handle them and may be a little irritable. It is even more important at this time, that you stay within your love and your light. Try not to be negatively affected by others. If this happens, send out love to that soul and walk upon your own sacred journey. Mother Earth will be experiencing many heightened energies in this next sphere of time. Stay strong, stay focused. Blessings to you, dear one.

Thank you Ashtar, Sananda and Michael

Wednesday, February 18, 2009

Greetings White Buffalo Calf Woman! Ashtar here. We see you taking back your power day by day. You must do this constantly and accept it as yours to move forward. We can see this as being most successful. Your sacred journey is just beginning. Walk in the present and be free of all others. Blessings to you, dear one.

Thank you Ashtar

Thursday, February 19, 2009

Greetings White Buffalo Calf Woman! Ashtar here with Sananda and Michael. We have something of the utmost importance to speak about with you today. Yes, your computer was shut down last night by us. I feel you were very alarmed by this so we wish to explain. There were others, shall we call them, that were very close to hacking through your computer. We cannot have them reading the material that you have saved. Therefore, we had to take some strong measures to get you off the computer. We would ask that you stay off that particular computer till further notice. We ask that you keep these communiqués to yourself. Do not add these to the files on the computer. We are watching closely and will tell you what is happening as opportunities unfold. Blessings to you, dear one.

Thank you Ashtar, Sananda and Michael

Saturday, February 21, 2009

Greetings White Buffalo Calf Woman! Ashtar here. We are all many beings from many galaxies; those who make up the Federation. We all bring a different perspective, so to speak, which makes up the totality. This too, is the way it is on your planet. Many souls, from different galaxies with a different perspective which makes up the totality. Hence the saying, "As above, so below." This topic was referred to in this communiqué, to show how it is always the correct way to follow your own truth; not that of others. Be free to be yourself without the o.k. of others. Do what is right for you and you will never be wrong. Keep reminding yourself of this; "Be free to be me". Blessings to you, dear one.

Thank you Ashtar

Sunday, February 22, 2009

Greetings White Buffalo Calf Woman! Ashtar here. It is written in time that we are not to ever doubt our heart where matters are concerned. Know that yours also tells of truth and will ever be so. It is getting easier for you to step away from 3-D reality but it is sometimes a struggle to stay in the higher dimensional way of thought. Know that we see you as the loving being you always have decided to reside as and will forever be so. Keep focused, dear one, in every moment, and it will become so much easier. Talk the talk, dear heart, but also walk the walk. Blessings to you, dear one.

Thank you Ashtar

Monday, February 23, 2009

Good morning; greetings White Buffalo Calf Woman! Ashtar here, once again, with Sananda and St. Germaine. We honour you this day, for your effort to stay within the positive mindset. As stated before, we realize this, at times, is difficult. We also know the true warrior you are and know you will overcome. We wish to speak also of gratitude. You always give gratitude for lessons learned and for gifts given. This is the true making of our Commander of Earth Ascension. Yes, you have much work ahead of you. Take this time to rest up; always enjoy yourself. Blessings to you, dear one.

Thank you Ashtar, Sananda and St. Germaine

Tuesday, February 24, 2009

Greetings White Buffalo Calf Woman, mother of all! Ashtar here, speaking of dreams. You know that the soul leaves the body in the sleeping stage and this is when it travels home for nourishment. It is at this time that the human mind thinks it is dreaming. It tricks the "self" into believing it is not real. As you well know, you had a "waking dream", shall I say, when of fact, you knew it was real, accepted it and even delighted in knowing where you went. These are going to become more apparent to you in the next while as you go on your nightly sojourn home. Enjoy! Blessings to you, dear one.

Thank you Ashtar

Wednesday, February 25, 2009

Greetings White Buffalo Calf Woman! Ashtar here. As you are quite aware, things are now moving in a forward motion. You can see evidence of this. Dear one, there is much more to come. We tell you to enjoy the ride. You are on a journey, dear one, that you could never have imagined! Blessings to you.

Thank you Ashtar

Thursday, February 26, 2009

Greetings White Buffalo Calf Woman, mother of all! Ashtar here with the Command present. Dear one, we are days away now. You have been most patient and all is about to be revealed. Sananda wishes to be present, so look forward to not only reuniting with the Command, but with the Spiritual Hierarchy also. Blessings to you, dear one!

Thank you Ashtar and the Command

Friday, February 27, 2009

Greetings White Buffalo Calf Woman! Ashtar here. Yes, we can have a question and answer session. You only have to ask, dear one. We hide nothing from you but cannot answer questions until they are asked. Please proceed.

From my prospective here on earth, I know I don't understand everything going on in regards to the ascension process. Am I correct in thinking that part of my "knowing of my mission" is being kept from me? And if so, will my awakening happen with all the others here on earth or before?

Ah, dear one, is the answer not in your heart? We have stressed this before, of following one's heart.

My heart tells me I am still "asleep" as far as my mission goes and that I will have to be awakened before others. It is just nice, sometimes, to have some validation from you on this matter and others.

And so it is. That is all. Now you have your validation.

Thank you. I do have another question I hope you will answer. Really, I have no feeling from my heart on this one, so maybe I'm not to know the answer yet. Will our mission start this year? Will the final ascension take place in 2012 or before? Actually, as far as the first question goes, I have an affirmative feel to this! It's the second question I wonder about.

Dear one, once again, we stress the feelings of heart. Why do you doubt so much? We understand you believe the big picture, the ascension process, and we know you believe in us or you would not bother speaking with us on a daily basis, for the most part. But, dear one, you have a very difficult time believing in yourself. We find this very sad indeed and this is where the most healing needs to take place with you. As for your questions, I will validate the first. Remember to work on your healing daily! Remember those who are coming around to help. Did I not say others will come? You see the evidence. The second question I cannot answer at this time; it all depends on humanity.

Thank you Ashtar. Yes, I know I struggle with who I am. I guess because I went through life, for the most part, feeling like an outcast, that I can't fathom me being "mother of all", teacher, healer, etc.

And, dear one, why was it you felt like an outcast? Maybe because you knew in your heart you didn't belong? That reason alone, I would think, would be a huge "aha" moment. Dear one, the life, the human life you have lived, is but a cake. Who you really are is the frosting on the cake. What is cake without the frosting? It is but a part of the whole that makes you who you are. You are many. You are here, you were there, you are in the future. Do you see now? And all need each other to move forward. I hope this has cleared away some of the cobwebs. Try to stay in the now and keep busy. Blessings to you, dear one.

Thank you Ashtar

Saturday, February 28, 2009

Greetings White Buffalo Calf Woman! Ashtar here. Yes, we understand from your viewpoint, that some lessons are hard to learn. But, dear one, that is what makes them worth learning! Wouldn't your life be very dull if you knew everything? Our dear lady, even I don't know everything! As I have stated before, your family members have their own agenda, their own paths to follow. Do you not realize by now that for the most part, your entire family does not have a foot on the path to ascension. And, because you do, well, I guess there is not much in common anymore. This is the way life works sometimes. It is not for you to judge others. These are big lessons but ones I know you are well on the way to learning. You, dear one, will always have emotions, but sometimes you just have to let them go. Blessings, dear one.

Thank you Ashtar

Sunday, March 1, 2009

Greetings White Buffalo Calf Woman! Ashtar here with Sananda. And so it is! The email has been sent. Now it is for the other dear soul to decide what is best now. For you see, everyone has freewill. Will she work with you or will she be overcome with fear of what she may be getting herself into? Time will only tell. Thank you, dear one, for contacting this one. You are stepping forward into your true self. Blessings to you, dear one.

Thank you Ashtar and Sananda

Monday, March 2, 2009

Greetings White Buffalo Calf Woman! Ashtar here. We once again are moving forward to a new plateau in the journey of ascension. You will feel the new energies surrounding you, at a faster pace. Remember, it does not just affect you, but everyone, person and animal, living in your space.

Know it for what it is. We shall speak more on this topic in the days to come. Blessings to you, dear one.

Thank you Ashtar

Tuesday, March 3, 2009

Greetings White Buffalo Calf Woman! Ashtar here with St. Germaine and Sananda. We wish to speak today of your mission. We hear you and Daniel talking quite often of the how's and when's of this event taking place. Dear one's, do you not realize you are on your missions and always have been? Your aura's give off quite an energy of peace and quiet that others are drawn to. Do you have another added layer to your mission such as teaching? What is in the heart? An extraordinary affirmation, we know. Yes, we will validate this for you as well as the RV. Yes, the second layer, or we can call it, level of your mission, will begin soon. It will pertain to readying the souls of earth to our imminent arrival. From there, we will work together to teach others of the higher energies, who will ascend, what to expect in their new dimension and how it will pertain to the whole. New technologies, new ways of growing food and how to sustain a clean, environmentally friendly earth, will be taught. We will not come forth at this time with all the components of what part your mission will be in all this, but of course, it is something that you already know of. We did want to give you some info, so as to answer some of the questions at this time. Blessings to you, dear one.

Thank you for the info, Ashtar, St. Germaine and Sananda

Friday, March 6, 2009

Greetings White Buffalo calf Woman! Ashtar speaking. We watch and wait and are available to answer any questions you may have. The one that seems to be on your mind this day is the question of whether you and Daniel are so-called "earth allies". On a certain level, yes you are but not in the sense of the communiqué you are speaking of. You are of a higher consciousness than that! My lady, you are "galactic royalty"! You know who you are and are accepting of this. You acknowledge the many white feathers. They are sacred. Keep them in your heart always. You will remember your purpose. It will come. Blessings to you, dear one.

Thank you Ashtar

Saturday, March 7, 2009

Ashtar, this morning, while reading a communiqué, it became clear to me that I also blame myself for the Federation not showing in our atmosphere. I have been living one foot in the third/fourth dimension as Nancy Horn and doing things that she would do, and the other foot in the higher dimensions as White Buffalo Calf Woman. I realize that it is time to make a very hard decision (for my mind) and go with my heart to the higher dimensions. My "earth family", of course, is not any less important than the rest of the world; they are all one and should be treated as such. Therefore, I cannot get caught up in the dramas anymore; their decisions on family matters have to be their own. It is time to awaken; lets do what we were sent here to do. Thank you for your time and for listening to me.

Ah, dear one, that was quite a statement. We see a burden has been lifted from you. We have been sending you subtle hints for some time now as we could not interfere in your free will. Now you have set yourself free from your earthly shackles, we are now free to come forward with help. You know who you are and will now receive visits from us. We will, together, decide on the best way to move forward. Blessings to you, dear mother of all. I'm sure you feel our excitement.

Thank you Ashtar

Wednesday, March 11, 2009

Greetings White Buffalo Calf Woman! Sananda here. Today we will speak of the importance of family. You have been a little on edge lately as far as getting too involved with family. They are your earth family; nothing wrong with being involved, just do not let their beliefs become your beliefs. Walk your own path, that is all. Your troubling times are almost at an end. You can now look forward to a joyous future. Blessings to you, dear one.

Thank you Sananda

Thursday, March 12, 2009

Greetings White Buffalo Calf Woman! Ashtar here. Greetings, once again, it has been awhile. You are going through a time now when everything around you is in upheaval. This needs to play itself out to come to a most agreeable outcome. You will then be able to come to terms with what needs to be taken care of before our arrival. Blessings to you, dear one, and don't forget those around you who are more than willing to help.

Thank you Ashtar

Saturday, March 14, 2009

Greetings White Buffalo Calf Woman. Ashtar here, speaking today of negative energies. Dear one, these are energies of the darker spectrum that you are trying to lighten. The only job you can do is lighten the situation and go from there. That is your job, nothing more, nothing less. As you know, not all can be on the same wavelength as you and you must let them go on their way. You are our goddess of the buffalo and absolutely know what to do in every situation. Blessings to you, dear one.

Thank you Ashtar

Sunday, March 15, 2009

Greetings White Buffalo Calf Woman! Ashtar here with news of a grand reunion. We have been making some final decisions and can now tell you the time is very near, almost upon you. We know you will be pleased at this announcement. Get your RV ready! The teachings will begin in earnest.

This is a positive go. We know it has been most difficult at times and we have learned a lot about human consciousness, the human psyche and how it all ties in together. We, the Federation, thank you so much for what you have gone through on behalf of us. Blessings, dear one.

Thank you Ashtar

Monday, March 16, 2009

Greetings White Buffalo Calf Woman! Ashtar here with Lord Michael. Very soon we will be making our appearance into your atmosphere, in a way that will not alarm you. It is time for you to remember your teachings. You will remember those in which to contact. You will be traveling extensively around the globe of Mother Earth. We have told you that your time will not be your own for long stretches of time. We wish to thank you for your patience in this matter as there were some outside forces that had to be seen to. Blessings to you, dear one.

Thank you Ashtar and Lord Michael

It is wise for you and Daniel to get your affairs in order. This is Ashtar. By this I mean organize your premises for leaving long periods at a time. Do not leave food that will spoil, etc. Tidy the apartment, if you must. Thank you for accepting this communiqué at such short notice. Blessings, dear ones.

Thank you Ashtar

Tuesday, March 17, 2009

Greetings White Buffalo Calf Woman! Ashtar here. We have commented on the actual timeline for you to begin your teachings. Let me say at this time, it is only days away. This is why I have asked you both to get your affairs in order; just enough so that you may leave for a few weeks at a time. You already know of what your teachings will consist of; it is just a matter of the veil being lifted. Your teachings do consist of getting humanity ready for our imminent arrival. We trust in this happening according to our laws. Thank you, dear ones and blessings to you.

Thank you Ashtar

Wednesday, March 18, 2009

Greetings White Buffalo Calf Woman! Ashtar here with greetings of returning home, to your true self. You will be feeling the energies exponentially and will be changing and learning by the day. This so called "sickness" you are feeling, is in actuality, a letting go of "stuff" that does not serve your purpose. When it is all said and done, you will be a whole new woman. Blessings to you, dear one!

Thank you Ashtar

Thursday, March 19, 2009

Greetings White Buffalo Calf Woman! Ashtar here. One by one, the blankets of isolation that surround your planet will be lifted and First Contact, as others wish to call it, will be made. This event will occur very soon. We need you and Daniel to be ready at a moments notice. Blessings, dear one.

Thank you Ashtar

Saturday, March 21, 2009

Greetings White Buffalo Calf Woman! Ashtar here. Today we will speak of the magnetic field. This is not something everyone is aware of during their day to day lives. It is, for all intents and purposes, something that one just lives with. Therefore, when it is lifted, there will be a sense, for some, of their world slightly out of kilter. As stated before, personalities will differ from a "high" feeling to that of "depression". If any of these arise in others, know it for what it is. We are so close now, dear one. Days away.

Enjoy your remaining days; with not much to do, just relax. All is well. Blessings to you, dear one.

Thank you Ashtar

Tuesday, March 24, 2009

Greetings White Buffalo Calf Woman! Ashtar here. Even though it does not seem so, everything is progressing nicely along. We wish not to shake the boat, so to speak, so for now you are at your families. This will move along quickly and then the time is yours to teach. Blessings, dear one.

Thank you Ashtar

Friday, March 27, 2009

Don't know if I should be speaking today as my heart is heavy and I don't seem to be as involved as I once was. Most days I don't care to be. I'm tired of living like a caged animal. I thought I would have had the knowledge to move forward with my teachings by now. I'm forever being told "soon, soon" but soon never seems to come.

Greetings, dear one. Ashtar here. I have noticed, for quite a few months now, that your light has been diminishing. We are very sorry for this as I know it has been frustrating for you. We have been telling you "soon" as to keep you going forward on your path. We see now we cannot keep doing this. It will have to now be your decision.

My decision to what? Keep on a lonely path going nowhere? You may see things differently from your vantage point, but here, one day turns into the next without anything changing. I try to stay positive hoping for at least our vehicle to be back on the road. I'm sorry for complaining, but really, WHY DO I FEEL THAT I WAS SUPPOSE TO QUIT MY JOB?

Dear one, at the time you had a journey to take; one that required you to quit your job. And everything since has led you here to this place. It may not be what you had in mind but you have lessons to learn. You have had many "troubles" as you call them; we like to label them lessons.

Your hardships are truly almost over. If you can hang in there for awhile longer, I promise they will be finished. This is your decision. We don't like to see you this way as you know you are a treasured member of the Federation who chose to go down to have a "human experience". You do have teachings that you will eventually remember when the time is right. We hope and pray you will continue on your mission but according to the laws of freewill, it must be your decision. Please think positively on this. Blessings to you, dear one.

Thank you Ashtar

Friday, March 27, 2009 (con't)

Greetings, White Buffalo Calf Woman! Ashtar here, once again. We, of the Command, wish you to know you still have your mission of teaching, which will begin this year, but the time is not yet upon us. We do not want any thoughts of desertion; we would never do this, as you are an important part of the whole ascension process. We understand you miss being around the aboriginal community and are rectifying this. Please be patient as we also have to follow a certain schedule pertaining to this. We do wish for you to go back to meditation on a full time basis, meaning everyday, and continue to channel. Blessings, dear one.

Thank you Ashtar

Saturday, March 28, 2009

Greetings White Buffalo Calf Woman! Ashtar here with Lord Sananda, who wishes to say a few words. Blessings, dearest heart, Lord Sananda speaking. Surround yourself with the love you know is coming your way. You should never fear that which is your destiny. This is the time, my heart, that you should be enjoying and celebrating the time you have left with your earth family. Your old mission, shall we say, is coming to a closing and both you and Daniel will start on your new missions of teaching others. This has not started as of yet, as the timing is not yet right. Yes, your reconnection to us will be this year, the year of 2009. This will be a joyous event for all to see. Shall we say a "worldwide event". We have played your visions over and over and have added a few ourselves to make an event that will never be forgotten. Keep the love and the light burning strong. The time will soon be upon us. Blessings of love to you, dearest heart.

Thank you Lord Sananda and Ashtar

Sunday, March 29, 2009

Greetings White Buffalo Calf Woman! Ashtar here. Your assumptions are correct; you are one and the same. The reason for you being on this plane of existence, is for the experience and for making your way through the darkness to the light, where you realize who you are. Just relax; always things are going according to plan and you are always on the correct pathway. We wish to reunite soon; please look for us in your skies and feel us in your home. You are beginning to see flashes of us and this will proceed till you can fully see us. Blessings to you, dear one.

Thank you Ashtar

Sunday March 29, 2009 (con't)

Greetings White Buffalo Calf Woman! Ashtar here, once again. It seems that it is almost upon us for a short visit to the earths atmosphere. This will be very brief and we will make sure you see us and recognize us for who we are. The Federation and the Command are very pleased with the progress made on earth. The light is ever expanding and it is time we made an appearance to thank our earth allies. And so it is. Blessings to you, dear one.

Thank you Ashtar

Wednesday, April 1, 2009

Greetings White Buffalo Calf Woman! Ashtar here. There are times, in ones life, when one feels maybe a little trapped. Like living in a box where one cannot escape. This is what is happening for you at this time. This is for you to heal the self in order to continually raise your vibration. This is in preparation for your mission which must start this year. You are going through many aches and pains; just remember you are not "sick", just transforming. When this phase is complete, it will be easy sailing on forward. Blessings to you, dear one.

Thank you Ashtar

Thursday, April 2, 2009

Greetings White Buffalo Calf Woman! Ashtar here with many greetings of love for you from family, friends and colleagues. The time is soon upon us for "First Contact" as we will call it. Daniel has had a certain dream. You have had dreams; now combine the two together. When you have met us on the earth plane, you will be invited onto the ship for your grand awakening. We have to tell you at this time, the two of you will not be returning to the earth plane the same people. You will look somewhat the same but because of your new knowledge, or should I say, forgotten knowledge, your spiritual self will be different as well as the way you portray yourself to others. And your missions will begin. Blessings to you, dear one!

Thank you Ashtar

Thursday, April 9, 2009

Greetings White Buffalo Calf Woman! Ashtar here. It has been awhile since our last communiqué and much has taken place in a short time. We are somewhat ready for a short visit into your atmosphere and you, dear one, are somewhat ready to receive us. Shall we both say "We are as ready as we'll ever be"? All must go forward from a specific starting point and we are at that starting point now in this time frame. It will be good to see you again, my friend and colleague. We are planning a light show for everyone's benefit and then they will briefly see one of our fleet. It cannot be mistaken who has put on the show. Others on your planet will step forward and say it was manufactured by their hands but the truth will come out. That is all that matters in the end. Blessings to you, dear one.

Thank you Ashtar

Wednesday, April 15, 2009

Greetings White Buffalo Calf Woman! Ashtar here. It has been awhile since our last communiqué. Every trial you are going through at this time, is for the betterment of your consciousness. These struggles will soon come to an end for you and I promise, once again, that everything that is your hearts desire, will be yours. This space was also given to you as a time to reflect upon the past and to project your hopes for the future. You have been putting this to good use. The rough times are almost over. Blessings to you, dear one.

Thank you Ashtar

Tuesday, April 21, 2009

Greetings White Buffalo Calf Woman! Ashtar here, checking in for our weekly communiqué. For the most part, we are now playing a waiting game, on your earth plane and within our space in time. We hope to have news very soon but wish for both you and Daniel to keep doing your best. We are always around should either one of you need to talk. Blessings to you, dear one.

Thank you Ashtar

Tuesday, April 28, 2009

Greetings White Buffalo Calf Woman! Ashtar here with greetings from the Command. We see a peacefulness and calmness coming over you that was previously not there. For that, we are very grateful. As with all other situations, do not think of negative outcomes, but think positively and you will manifest that into existence. As with yesterdays situation, you thought positively and the outcome was of a positive nature. It really is that simple. Live in the moment. Blessings to you, dear one.

Thank you Ashtar

Saturday, May 2, 2009

Greetings White Buffalo Calf Woman! Ashtar here. We are in the midst of crunch time. Everything will be happening rather quickly now. It will start in the morning with your meditation with Red Cloud. Be extremely aware of everything he tells you for he will be working with you quite extensively. Your time is here, dear one! Live and learn! Be bold and go forward, where no woman has gone before! We are ever by your side. Blessings to you, dear one.

Thank you Ashtar

Monday, May 25, 2009

Greetings White Buffalo Calf Woman! Ashtar here. So good to be communicating once again. Dear one, it will all be coming about shortly; nothing like you have expected, but all the same, a most rewarding, exciting time. Go about your final days as you normally would. I shall be most pleased to see you once again shortly Blessings, dear one.

Thank you Ashtar

Wednesday, May 27, 2009

Greetings White Buffalo Calf Woman! Ashtar here with greetings from friends and family from beyond. Rest up, dear one, as you have a lot to remember from the higher realms. When you return to earth, it will be yours to teach. So, much rest for now. Blessings to you, dear one.

Thank you Ashtar

Tuesday, June 2, 2009

Greetings White Buffalo Calf Woman! Ashtar here. Thank you for answering my call. Dear one, it is only days now before we see one another again. This, I did want to check in and remind you of again. Blessings to you, dear one.

Thank you Ashtar

Tuesday, June 9, 2009

Greetings White Buffalo Calf Woman! Ashtar here once again. This time that is approaching, is one for rebalancing. I ask of you, more cleansing and more meditation please. Lets try to, once again, get back to a routine that you kept a couple of years back. Stay centered within yourself and do not take on the so called "troubles" of others. This is a good starting place. Blessings to you, dear one.

Thank you Ashtar

Wednesday, June 10, 2009

Greetings White Buffalo Calf Woman! Ashtar here. Energies are swirling so close for a start to your "new" life. Dear one, it really will be beyond your wildest dreams. You see the difference in your skies and an overwhelming feeling of peace; letting it all go and letting the chips fall were they may. This, dear one, is truly living in the moment. Blessings to you, dear one.

Thank you Ashtar

Thursday, June 11, 2009

Greetings White Buffalo Calf Woman! Ashtar here with many greetings from above. It takes some time to change things; your technology, spirituality, banking systems; everything must crash to start anew. Keep your visions alive in your mind as that is how to go forward with your mission and to help the new world. Always remember, dear one, you are an integral part of the Federation. Blessings to you, dear one.

Thank you Ashtar

Sunday, June 13, 2009

Greetings White Buffalo Calf Woman! Ashtar here. We have come to a culmination of all that can be learned on the earth plane and is now time to take that step forward. Your "dreamtime" has been a "mumble jumble", shall we say, of images and stories that do not make any sense. It is now time for you to return to the ship, in your dreamtime, to progress with your teachings. My, but it is good to be communicating on a daily basis with you again. I would like to say also, we feel you are most ready, as we have had our "spies" watching. Yes, you have noticed who they are; you see, dear one, your discernment is becoming quite sharp. You have progressed more than you think and we are quite pleased. Thank you for your patience in this matter. Blessings to you, dear one.

Thank you Ashtar

Sunday, June 14, 2009

Greetings White Buffalo Calf Woman! Ashtar here with greetings from the Federation as a whole. Much has been accomplished upon earth and we send out a big "thank you" to all our ground members. If not for the ground crew, we would not be in the fortunate circumstances we see ourselves in now. In fact, we now find ourselves ahead of our predicted schedule. We send out waves of gratitude. What we have deemed "First Contact", can now happen ahead of schedule and we say it will not be long now. We see some of you are becoming what you would call "homesick" and are longing to be with us again. This fills our hearts with joy; the love emanating from many dear souls upon earth. We can promise you it will not be long now, for we miss you as you miss us. Dear one, blessings to you.

Thank you Ashtar

Monday, June 15, 2009

Greetings White Buffalo Calf Woman! Ashtar here. The rate of energy surrounding you is rising every day. It will soon reach a peak where your desires will start to manifest. Keep within the moment; no worries, no fears. All is well. Blessings to you, dear one.

Thank you Ashtar

Tuesday, June 16, 2009

Greetings White Buffalo Calf Woman! Ashtar here! Energy flowing and always making way for the new. This is the way it is to be. To make way for the new, we must make room, therefore letting go of the old. Blessings to you, dear one.

Thank you Ashtar

Thursday, June 18, 2009

Greetings White Buffalo Calf Woman! Ashtar here with greetings from the Federation. The Spiritual Hierarchy is present with us this morning. Welcome, dear one! It is almost upon us, this grand re-awakening of many of our ground forces. You will be the ones to go forth out to the masses with news of our existence and why we are here in this pivotal moment in time. We ask that you go forth as warriors and be diligent in your teachings. This is most important. We are in awe of the work that has been done. Thank you, most graciously. And I, Ashtar signing off also. Blessings, dear one.

Thank you Ashtar and the Spiritual Hierarchy

Greetings White Buffalo Calf Woman! Ashtar here. When you are feeling a little out of sorts, it is best to go into a room by yourself and return to centre; take a few deep breaths and let everything go. The energy is getting quite strong now as well as so many different energies converging at once. Take care of yourself first. Blessings to you, dear one.

Thank you Ashtar

Friday, June 26, 2009

Greetings, White Buffalo Calf Woman! Ashtar here. We have been beside you, dear one, these last few days. No one seems to listen to anything you have to say. You do know the answer why. In the "big scheme" of your earthly family, it seems your opinions mean very little. It is up to you, because of freewill, to find your path and travel it. Sometimes it is a lonely path but one that brings the heart much needed peace. You have the choice, dear one. Thank you for your time with me this day. Blessings to you.

Thank you Ashtar

Saturday, July 4, 2009

Greetings White Buffalo Calf Woman! Ashtar here with greetings from above. The Federation asks that you take this time to look after yourself; you are letting go of a lot of that which no longer serves you. Stay strong as you are; it will soon be over. We are always with you and at watch over all and will very soon be seen in great numbers through your skies. Keep positive, dear one. Blessings to you.

Thank you Ashtar

Monday, July 20, 2009

Greetings White Buffalo Calf Woman! Ashtar here. The time is now and the energies seem to be spinning out of control. Stay in the now; keep looking upwards. We are here. Blessings to you, dear one.

Thank you Ashtar

Friday, July 24, 2009

Greetings White Buffalo Calf Woman! Ashtar here. Thought it was time we caught up on a few things. First, I am extremely pleased on how you are handling the energies surrounding you. Secondly, you will start to see forms soon. By forms, I mean human forms; they will be a little cloudy at first but at some point will start to take shape and you will eventually see facial expression, etc. Do not be alarmed. They are present to help you. You have come such a long way in a short period of time. Dear one, I know you can't possibly understand what you have been through, but all will be revealed at a later date. At times it feels to you that you have completely given up but this is not the case. This is simply the lull before "full steam ahead". Dear one, blessings to you.

Thank you Ashtar

Friday, July 31, 2009

Greetings White Buffalo Calf Woman! Ashtar here with many greetings from family, friends and colleagues. The time has come to quit worrying about whether you did some good in this lifetime. You have made enormous progress and many dear souls come to know your light. This is one of the reasons we deem to show ourselves very, very soon. Keep talking and thanking the "shadow" people you see, as soon they will present themselves as your guardians. Both you and Daniel are to be awakened soon as per your mission. From the Ashtar Command Fleet and, of course, myself, thank you for all you have accomplished on your mission thus far. Dear one, we've only just begun! Blessings and love to you both.

Thank you Ashtar

Wednesday, August 5, 2009

Good evening White Buffalo Calf Woman! Ashtar here. Please keep your spirits up; this is not doing you or us any good. We know you are tired of waiting but the final say on First Contact is not solely up to us. The Creator has the final say and when it's a go, it will happen. Keep doing what you have been; living in the moment. Blessings to you.

Thank you Ashtar

Sunday August 9, 2009

Good afternoon White Buffalo Calf Woman! Ashtar here with news of the upcoming storm. It will be massive in size, no worries. All part of the process. Keep positive as something new and wonderful is on the horizon. Blessings to you, dear one.

Thank you Ashtar

Sunday, August 30, 2009

Good evening! This is Ashtar speaking. At this point, we really do not know what to do next. We have been trying our hardest to awaken you, with no results.

Good evening White Buffalo Calf Woman! Ashtar here. Thank you for stopping that communication. It was I who rang but somehow another has gotten through. It will be dealt with. I wish to speak to you of your feelings. You have had quite a lot going on, dear one and it is natural to feel the way you do. This is the natural flow of grieving. Just give it time. You have seen your father and know he is o.k. As for your dear beloved Sammi Girl, she is well also, as you have noticed in your dreamtime. Dear one, you have done that dear friend a huge favor in letting her go. It is hard on you, yes, but keep strong and keep the faith that all is well. We shall meet very, very soon. Dear one, let the party begin. Blessings to you.

Thank you Ashtar

Monday, September 21, 2009

Greetings White Buffalo Calf Woman! Ashtar Here. So good to communicate once again. Shall we start over and try a daily dialogue once more? I feel it is time once again for this, as time is collapsing upon itself and the changes will happen soon. Stay in a positive state of mind at all times as this time is crucial. Dear one, you and I have been in communication for some time now through what you call channeling. Know that soon this will be face to face upon the grandest reunion of all times! Blessings to you, dear one.

Thank you Ashtar

Tuesday, September 22, 2009

Greetings White Buffalo Calf Woman! Ashtar here. We have safely arrived into this 3D reality. We are keeping a careful watch over possible confrontations but hope all stays quiet. We are so excited to finally be amongst you in this reality in time and for the grand reality. It is finally happening, dear one, where as other times we have had to postpone our mission time and time again. Dear one, blessings to you and I will keep you on a daily update as to what is happening.

Thank you Ashtar

Wednesday, September 23, 2009

Greetings White Buffalo Calf Woman! Ashtar here with greetings from within the 3D world. I feel the joy coming from within your soul at the thought of our nearness. This will be a short communiqué this day as we have many preparations for what is to take place very shortly. Let it be said to all on the 3D earth plane, "The change is in the wind". Blessings to you, dear one.

Thank you Ashtar

Thursday, September 24, 2009

Greetings White Buffalo Calf Woman! Ashtar here. Things are progressing nicely and all is on track. I must say, it is good to be in communication with you once again. I feel the need to teach beating within your heart centre. The opportunity will definitely present itself shortly. Keep the heart fires burning, dear one. Blessings to you.

Thank you Ashtar

Friday, September 25, 2009

Greetings White Buffalo Calf Woman! Ashtar here with greetings from a place in time right in the general vicinity. The wings of change move ever forward in time, soon to meet up with destiny. Enjoy the time that you have now as it cannot last past the time in which your destiny meets up with you and the veils come off those whose missions must be met. Dear one, blessings to you.

Thank you Ashtar

Sunday, September 27, 2009

Greetings White Buffalo Calf Woman! Ashtar here. I was right at your side today; what a wonderful celebration for our animal friends. I am most pleased that the shampooing system works well. Your little Nicky thanks you. Of course, Sammi was with us today; I know you felt her presence. All is well over the Rainbow Bridge for all animals. Dear one, it is true; they all wait patiently for their loved ones. As for the mission, still on track for a wonderful outcome. Keep looking to the skies! Blessings to you.

Thank you Ashtar

Monday, September 28, 2009

Greetings White Buffalo Calf Woman! Ashtar here. We are gathering in numbers for the final "thrust" to rid the earth of all darkness before they cause anymore grief…is the mission of the moment. Thereafter, it will not be long, dear one, before everything else falls into place. Keep on living in the moment. Reading seems to keep you in this vibration, so by all means continue, but remember to call on me every day for a general update. Dear one, blessings to you.

Thank you Ashtar

Tuesday, September 29, 2009

Greetings White Buffalo Calf Woman! Ashtar here. It is always best to stay in the now moment even when speaking with others. Let others play out their dramas and scenarios. This way you keep your eye on what will happen for yourself. Always keep your wants and needs within your thoughts for us to listen to. Dear one, the time moves ever faster and it will be very soon, you and I will meet again. Blessings to you, dear one.

Thank you Ashtar

Wednesday, September 30, 2009

Greetings White Buffalo Calf Woman! Ashtar here. The time is slipping along and once into October, things will really start to pick up. The energies have been swirling even higher these past couple of days. This is why you are so tired, trying to integrate the new energy and light into your body. Rest when this happens. Blessings to you, dear one.

Thank you Ashtar

Thursday, October 1, 2009

Greetings White Buffalo Calf Woman! Ashtar here. As you realize, we must protect the people of earth from the last of the dark ones who still have power. They are becoming fewer and fewer every day. For this reason, we are planning some fly-bys or decloakings, whatever one may want to call this experience. We will start with a few and increase in numbers as we can allow. Dear one, these are exciting times and we wish for all to enjoy these precious moments leading up to our grand reunion. Blessings to you, dear one.

Thank you Ashtar

Friday, October 2, 2009

Greetings White Buffalo Calf Woman! Ashtar here. We gaze around your planet and are always in awe of the many who are awakening and those who are becoming curious. The light shining radiantly from many, makes ones heart sing with joy. You are to be commended for coming such a long way in so short of a time space. We long to reunite, dear one, and with our plans in place, this is coming to fruition quicker than once possible. Dear one, blessings to you.

Thank you Ashtar

Saturday, October 3, 2009

Greetings White Buffalo Calf Woman! Ashtar here with greetings from the starship. Once we are able to land is when the real work begins. That is when we must stand together as a united front to teach those who are afraid, of our mission. We hope to bring a great many on board with us, who otherwise, would not know of what may be happening in their world. Dear one, rest and be prepared for the work that must be done. Blessings to you, dear one.

Thank you Ashtar

Sunday, October 4, 2009

Greetings White Buffalo Calf Woman! Ashtar here. We hover above and beyond, yet we see all taking place on earth. The timelines continue to press together till the time when your "linear time" will be non existent. We tend to call this a collapsing and most people on earth are privy to what is going on, whether consciously or unconsciously. Dear one, the time draws near for some major changes for all of humanity. As you well know, some will welcome it, others will be bound in fear. The huge job will be to try and alleviate the fear amongst the masses. Blessings to you, dear one!

Thank you Ashtar

Monday, October 5, 2009

Greetings White Buffalo Calf woman! Ashtar here. We are, for the moment, constantly doing work on and within the earth. I could describe in technical detail exactly what it is that's happening, but I'm afraid at the moment, it is too technical for you to understand. Dear one, soon the teachings will begin in earnest. It is time for our presence to be known to all. This will be a trying time but we will be assured great success. Dear one, blessings to you.

Thank you Ashtar

Tuesday, October 6, 2009

Greetings White Buffalo Calf Woman! Ashtar here with many greetings from many friends from the higher realms. All journeys must end when new ones begin. Both you and Daniel's journeys are about to start anew with a new earthly galactic school room. Be prepared. This will happen soon. Blessings to you, dear one.

Thank you Ashtar

Wednesday, October 7, 2009

Greetings White Buffalo Calf Woman! Ashtar here. As it is late in your timeline, I will not keep you. Only know, that you will soon see evidence of us in your skies. And so begins a story……
Blessings to you, dear one.

Thank you Ashtar

Thursday, October 8, 2009

Greetings White Buffalo Calf Woman! Ashtar here. Forever we move forward in our mission, gaining momentum as time goes by into timelessness. Keep on being in the moment as time progresses and we make a formal announcement. Blessings to you, dear one.

Thank you Ashtar

Friday, October 9, 2009

Greetings White Buffalo Calf Woman! Ashtar here. It is good to see Daniel tracking us each day on his "Google" radar! So much happening at this end, at the moment. Our dates will manufacture themselves in your timeline quite quickly. Dear one, stay tuned to the skies. Blessings to you.

Thank you Ashtar

Monday, October 12, 2009

Greetings White Buffalo Calf Woman! Ashtar here. We have heard you speak of the mass landings, Nesara and even the announcements. The announcements will be made this year, as well as Nesara. The mass landings will be in the first part of 2010. This has been known to us for awhile now and now is known to you. Preparations should start now, dear one. Blessings to you.

Thank you Ashtar

There will be much to accomplish in the years leading up to 2012. Very, very busy!

Tuesday, October 13, 2009

Greetings White Buffalo Calf Woman! Ashtar here. We shall come shortly after our deal is complete. That was our agreement and we, the Federation, will stick to this. You have come a long way in a short time and continue to progress, doing what is good for the self. Blessings to you, dear one.

Thank you Ashtar

Wednesday, October 14, 2009

Greetings White Buffalo Calf Woman! Ashtar here. Ah, the excitement! You are almost bursting with it! At this time, I must ask you to do some daily meditation, Daniel also. It gives us a little more opportunity to work with you quietly without distractions. The time is ever drawing near. Blessings to you, dear one.

Thank you Ashtar

Thursday, October 15, 2009

Greetings White Buffalo Calf Woman! Ashtar here. Once again, we begin our morning meditations. This will be a regular occurrence until your particular mission begins and the veil is lifted. We have mush to accomplish in a short time. During your meditation, I wish for you to bring yourself to the ship. Blessings to you, dear one.

Thank you Ashtar

Friday, October 16, 2009

Greeting White Buffalo Calf Woman! Ashtar here from the official office of the Hierarchy, aboard the New Jerusalem. It is not for me to say how one should be feeling or acting at this time, as everyone is quite different. At this time, some are quite excited at the possibilities and others are quite frightened of the prospects. This is where my wonderful ground crew comes into play, as a positive light into the situation playing out on Mother Earth. This is a time for prayers and good will to your fellow man. Blessings to you, dear one.

Thank you Ashtar

Saturday, October 17, 2009

Greetings White Buffalo Calf Woman! Ashtar here. These past couple of days you have been with us here, finalizing plans for your mission. Your mission is quite detailed in its entirety and involves mush traveling; hence the downtime for this past year. Please eat more roughage; fruits and vegetables. Blessings to you, dear one.

Thank you Ashtar

Sunday, October 18, 2009

Greetings White Buffalo Calf Woman! Ashtar here with greetings from the starship crew. Today we are finalizing and tying up a few details pertaining to that which will be happening in your timeline very shortly. Dear one, you have received your news this morning along with Daniel; confirmation of your vision, which will happen at a later date. A grand reunion and party it will be! Blessings to you, dear one.

Thank you Ashtar

Monday, October 19, 2009

Greetings White Buffalo Calf Woman! Ashtar here. Thank you for keeping up the meditation. Anytime you have any questions while here, please ask. Blessings to you, dear one.

Thank you Ashtar

Tuesday, October 20, 2009

Greetings White Buffalo Calf Woman! Ashtar here. The energies are in themselves, swirling and quickening ever faster! Try to keep a clear mind, dear one. We, of the High Council, understand this is very difficult but you are persisting quite well. Blessings to you, dear one.

Thank you Ashtar and High Council

Wednesday, October 21, 2009

Greetings White Buffalo Calf Woman! Ashtar here. The negativity that has been surrounding the planet has long been dismantled. There are just a few souls who need to be rounded up and all will be a go. The mass sightings will begin very soon. Dear one, stay tuned to the skies. Blessings to you.

Thank you Ashtar

Thursday, October 22, 2009

Greetings White Buffalo Calf Woman! Ashtar here with greetings from many on the starship. The excitement builds with every moment here on board with the grand reunion, with many on the earth surface and those on our ship and all ships that surround the planet in love and peace. The buildup is almost as exciting as the actual reunion will be, do you not think? Many dear souls on the ground will welcome us once they see us and know we mean no harm. Dear one, keep forth your visions. Blessings to you.

Thank you Ashtar

Friday, October 23, 2009

Greetings White Buffalo Calf Woman! Ashtar here and you are most welcome. Ask and ye shall receive.! You have had a rather busy day so I will see you in meditation. Blessings to you, dear one.

Thank you Ashtar

Sunday, October 25, 2009

Greetings White Buffalo Calf Woman! Ashtar here with many golden greetings from those who miss you. Things will start to move along now as it is almost the end of your month October. We promise, this Xmas, there will be much to celebrate. When you have days that you seem to be generally "off", know that you are under the ministrations of the light beings. It is a long journey but most certainly well worth the feelings of generally being down. Blessings to you, dear one.

Thank you Ashtar

Monday, October 26, 2009

Greetings White Buffalo Calf Woman! Ashtar here with greetings from many. Today, I will discuss the mission and what it will involve. There are so many who do not understand who we are, why we come and what we have to offer other than the love and friendship we bring forth. This, of course, will be part of the mission, as you will remember who you are and you will remember how it is to live elsewhere. Of course, it won't hurt to show people that you have been living amongst them for years, with nothing to be afraid of. I know the energies are very hard on you at this time, dear one, but you will adapt to them. Take plenty of rest to absorb them internally. Blessings to you, dear one.

Thank you Ashtar

Tuesday, October 27, 2009

Greetings White Buffalo Calf Woman! Ashtar here. It is with great sadness, I must say, that we must wait just awhile longer for our reunion. Our missions we have on board, at this present time, are taking a little extra "time", as you would call it. This is not a massive delay, but all the same, it is a short delay. Nothing to worry over. Other than the short delay, things are moving into place. Blessings to you, dear one.

Wednesday, October 28, 2009

Greetings White Buffalo Calf Woman! Ashtar here with greetings from aboard. We shall start off with yesterdays message; not to worry, not long of a wait. We are, as they say, ending up with the arrests of the dark ones and from there on in, it will happen…123! Blessings to you, dear one.

Thank you Ashtar

Thursday, October 29, 2009

Greetings White Buffalo Calf Woman! Ashtar here. Keep holding on to your faith. You will see us in the skies soon. The finalization of the meetings are at hand and then the announcements. Blessings to you, dear one.

Thank you Ashtar

Friday, October 30, 2009

Greetings White Buffalo Calf Woman! Ashtar here. We must begin to work strictly upon the energy around you and within you. This must be done on a daily basis with your infinity breath and clearing the chakras. Only then will you start vibrating at a higher level. Blessings to you, dear one.

Thank you Ashtar

Sunday, November 1, 2009

Greetings White Buffalo Calf Woman! Ashtar here and to answer your question, you would do fine. We understand, and I mean "we" of the higher realms, we understand how hard it is to live in the density that surrounds you and try to be the quiet, gentle soul that you are. Just keep upon your path and do exactly what you think is right in every circumstance. All will eventually fall into place. Blessings to you, dear one.

Thank you Ashtar

Monday, November 2, 2009

Greetings White Buffalo Calf Woman! Ashtar here with greetings from your many friends and colleagues. The time is now for more intense energies and many dreamtime memories. This all leading up to disclosure and consequently, to our mass landings and the official First Contact. All in divine timing. Blessings to you, dear one.

Tuesday, November 3, 2009

Greetings White Buffalo Calf Woman! Ashtar here. The energies of this, your month November, will be quite intense. Just let them come and quietly do their job. First Contact will be here very quickly as time speed is increasing. Drink plenty of water, as this seems to help you to integrate the energies better. Blessings to you, dear one.

Wednesday, November 4, 2009

Greetings White Buffalo Calf Woman! Ashtar here. Don't forget to drink plenty of water as it is important to the ascension. Just awhile longer dear one and blessings to you.

Thank you Ashtar

Thursday, November 5, 2009

Greetings White Buffalo Calf Woman! Ashtar here with great news! As we have stated, everything is on schedule, in fact, we may be able to move our date ahead. Wonderful news indeed. Get your earthly affairs in order, dear one, for we shall meet soon. Blessings to you.

Thank you Ashtar

Friday, November 6, 2009

Greetings White Buffalo Calf Woman! Ashtar here. We are stepping up preparations so that everyone has a very Merry Christmas on earth this year. There are so many fine details to put into play but will be accomplished. Keep the faith and keep in the moment. Blessings to you, dear one.

Thank you Ashtar

Sunday, November 8, 2009

Greetings White Buffalo Calf Woman! Ashtar here. This day begins with some disappointments.: realizing you have been in limbo for over a year. But, behind the scenes, something is happening that will make this past year seem like "child's play". Blessings to you, dear one.

Thank you Ashtar

Monday, November 9, 2009

Greetings White Buffalo Calf Woman! Ashtar here. Yes, First Contact is still slated for this year, 2009. Our mass landings will happen in the new year as stated beforehand. Blessings to you, dear one.

Thank you Ashtar

Tuesday, November 10, 2009

Greetings White Buffalo Calf Woman! Ashtar here. Keep your visions coming through music. They are very much quite clear to us. Keep the laughter; as they say "Laughter is the best medicine"! Blessings to you, dear one.

Thank you Ashtar

Wednesday, November 11, 2009

Greetings White Buffalo Calf Woman! Ashtar here on this famously wonderful date of your calendar year 2009....11:11! This is the beginning of a most magical time. Enjoy! Blessings to you, dear one.

Thank you Ashtar

Sunday, November 15, 2009

Greetings White Buffalo Calf Woman! Ashtar here and as Daniel says, "Today is the day"! Keep your ears and eyes open to the T.V. screen. Try to stay close to the apartment also. Blessings to you, dear one.

Thank you Ashtar

Tuesday, November 17, 2009

Greetings White Buffalo Calf Woman! Ashtar here with greetings from the Federation. You say that during our last communiqué, you were not able to detect anything on your T.V. screen. Dear one, you must learn to listen and decipher what you hear on T.V. You may miss some little detail that is very important! Things are progressing along and the time is quickly approaching. Blessings to you, dear one.

Thank you Ashtar and Federation

Wednesday, November 18, 2009

Greetings White Buffalo Calf Woman! Ashtar here. We are moving forward but I know it is usually unseen in your 3D reality. We continue to sing your praises, my little warrior, and soon we shall all meet again. Greetings to you, dear one.

Thank you Ashtar

Sunday, November 22, 2009

Greetings White Buffalo Calf Woman! Ashtar here. We will be seeing each other shortly; the mission must begin. It has been my decision to keep the small intricate details away from you, in your 3D reality, as it just causes much unnecessary confusion. I will say, that you will keep the apartment as a home base and you, Daniel and also Nick (when possible) will be doing quite a bit of traveling. This is all arranged for the new year 2010. As for your question, left ear, me; right ear, frequency testing. Blessings to you, dear one.

Thank you Ashtar

Wednesday, December 2, 2009

Greetings White Buffalo Calf Woman! Ashtar here. We have had a short delay as to give a few more the time to raise consciousness. It is still on schedule for announcements very soon. Keep grounded, dear one, and keep in the moment. Blessings to you.

Thank you Ashtar

Friday, December 4, 2009

Greetings White Buffalo Calf Woman! Ashtar here. Keep the faith; we are near and the announcements are soon! All to have a very Merry Christmas. Blessings to you, dear one.

Thank you Ashtar

Tuesday, December 29, 2009

Greetings White Buffalo Calf woman! Ashtar here with greetings from many who surround you at this time. The next few weeks will be very important; we need you in meditation for quietness. We understand the boredom you experience but please find time for what is important. There are those who wish to contact you. Thank you and blessings to you, dear one.

Thank you Ashtar

YEAR 2010

Friday, January 1, 2010

Greetings White Buffalo Calf Woman! Ashtar here. We have been sorting out, so to say, those who are ready to move forward in their endeavors. For you, dear one, the time is now. Meditate, be in the now, be in joy! Congratulations! Blessings to you, dear one.

Thank you Ashtar

Wednesday, January 6, 2010

Greetings White Buffalo Calf Woman! Ashtar here. Notice us in your skies for we are here. The truth will be out soon and everyone may start to live a joyful life. Blessings to you, dear one.

Thank you Ashtar

Wednesday, January 13, 2010

Greetings White Buffalo Calf Woman! Ashtar here. I am here to answer all questions you may have at this time.

I understand the statement about those who are on the path to ascension, need to learn to stay away from anything of a lower energy. Could you please explain if that pertains to family and friends? This relates to me.

Dear one, are you asking if you should stay away from your family and friends? If this is the question, I must ask you if you think they are of "dark energy"? Remember, "dark energy" is an energy that is extremely harmful to others, such as those that have taken another's life, those who purposely frighten others and deliberately inhibit them from a path of light, those that plunder Mother Earth knowingly and do not care. Now, you tell me, do your family and friends fall into this category?

No, I would think not.

Dear one, I may say, you do not have many "friends" on your plane of existence. You choose them very wisely and I see no problem at this time. You are a very good judge of character and need to realize this. Anyone negative coming within your space, you are right on top of it. Please remember, you have quite the "support system" around you, who would love a job to do. Just ask! You have many guides, many from the angelic realm and loved ones who are there to help. Send them love, ask them questions; you will get your answers. You are very good at seeing and acknowledging signs. You are also quite ready with a "Thank you"! This is all we ask; do not make it harder than it has to be. Just allow! Be in joy, smile, smile, smile! One other comment I would like to make pertaining to your question; you may be mistaking "dark lower energy" with fear. Those operating from the energy of fear, may at times, do and say things that you may not see as being of a "comfortable energy". Dear one, with all the loving, high energies bombarding earth right now, is it any wonder it is so frustrating to those who do not know of ascension. They do not understand why they feel this way and yes they feel the energy. It is what one chooses to do with the energy that is important. Just allow and be grateful and most of all, be in joy! Blessings to you, dear one.

Thank you Ashtar

Monday, January 25, 2010

Greetings White Buffalo Calf Woman! Ashtar here. There are those who wander the earth searching for the ultimate expression of themselves. For you, dear one, you have to look no further than what is right in front of your nose. The signs are so obvious; OPEN THOSE EYES WIDE AND SEE. You know the answer. Blessings to you, dear one.

Thank you Ashtar

Friday, February 26, 2010

Greetings, Ashtar here. It has been awhile since our last communiqué. It is taking much longer than we thought but everything is coming together quite nicely. It is quite expected, as things are progressing, that we can show ourselves this year so that all can come to a decision as to where and what they may want to go and do; the higher dimensions or to stay awhile longer in duality. Dear one, both you and I know where you are heading; just work on more meditation and trips to the ship. You are dearly missed by your pupils. I know this is a long, slow process, but enjoy it, for the real work is yet to come. Blessings to you, dear one.

Thank you Ashtar

Monday, March 8, 2010

Greetings White Buffalo Calf Woman! Ashtar here; it has been awhile. We are progressing ever closer to that which we, and the world, is waiting for; that one big party. We see more and more people have a gentle awakening every day. This does us good to see everything coming together as it should. It seems you have been waiting a long while within your given timeline. Rest assured, dear one, your dreams are coming to fruition. Thank you and blessings.

Thank you Ashtar

Sunday, March 14, 2010

Greetings, my lady! Aukmuk here. You are wondering why I have called upon you this night. Let me first explain that Ashtar has given me his signal this night, so that I may speak. My lady, thank you for waving to us in your skies. It is your way to acknowledge our love we are sending and we "blink" our love right back towards you. My lady, please ask to come to the ship in your dreamtime; you have been here lately and if you ask to remember, you will. My lady, it really is time for you to remember. We are here to help in this matter; all you do is ask. My lady, thank you for your time.

Thank you Aukmuk
Thank you Ashtar

Friday, March 19, 2010

Greetings White Buffalo Calf Woman! Ashtar here with many greetings from friends and past family members. Thank you for acknowledging us in your skies. Very soon, there will be a communiqué to you and Daniel, either on your television screen or your computer; depending which you have on at the time. It is very critical you both listen to this. It will be, in detail, what the next steps of your mission will be. At this time, I can only tell you, it is something very near and dear to your hearts. Till our communiqué, Ashtar signing off! Blessings to you, dear one.

Thank you Ashtar

Greetings, dear one! Archangel Michael here. Just adding a footnote to what Ashtar has communicated to you. My dear ones, have your suitcases packed; meaning, have your suitcases handy and ready to be packed! Blessings to you both with much love and gratitude.

Thank you Archangel Michael

Sunday, March 21, 2010

Greetings White Buffalo Calf Woman! Ashtar here with loving greetings. We are making headway this weekend; slowly but surely the dark see themselves as having lost the battle and are surely on their way out. We march ever forward in our duty to bring about love and peace to those who have done without for so long. Your body is healing from hundreds of years of living in and out of layers of negativity. You are mastering these layers quite fast and we are well pleased with your progress. Thank you for helping others along their way as that is the "galactic way"! Meditation will help the healing (also to Daniel). Blessings to you, dear one.

Thank you Ashtar

Thursday, March 25, 2010

Greetings White Buffalo Calf Woman! Ashtar here. We are making great gains and wish you to know we will be in touch quite soon. Ticking down the minutes! Blessings to you, dear one.

Thank you Ashtar

Friday, March 26, 2010

Greetings White Buffalo Calf Woman! Ashtar here with greetings from many, indeed! We shall start off our communiqué with a mention to the camera. My, is it getting a workout. Dan takes pictures and when he leaves for his JOB, then you take over the camera. Check the pictures closely; you just might find something. This is all leading up to the many "lights and objects" you are filming as of late. They are more frequent, are they not? And they will get even more so. We are bumping up our fly-bys, so that as many as possible can get used to our presence in the skies. We are hoping very, very soon, for our communiqué through the T.V. or computer screen. Sit tight, it will definitely happen. Blessings to you, dear one.

Thank you Ashtar

Sunday, April 4, 2010

Greetings White Buffalo Calf Woman! Ashtar here with many greetings from your "other" family. This is a time for pondering about that which is most important. You have so many who wish to help; just ask and allow! Blessings to you, dear one.

Thank you Ashtar

Friday, April 9, 2010

Greetings White Buffalo Calf Woman! Ashtar here. The time for moving forward is now. You will soon understand exactly what it is you have come to earth for at this time. We had a wondrous time on the ship this day, have we not? Everything coming together nicely. All is well. Blessings to you, dear one.

Thank you Ashtar

Tuesday, April 12, 2010

Greetings White Buffalo Calf Woman! Ashtar here with many greetings from friends and family. You are making great strides to move forward; coming into yourself, one might say. You are no longer letting anyone put you down, as in your energy, and you are listening more to your own voice and those of the higher realms who are looking out for your best interest. You are fast learning to shake off the outside world. We are moving in great strides forward and hope to be on your screen very soon. Blessings to you, dear one.

Thank you Ashtar

Saturday, April 16, 2010

Greetings White Buffalo Calf Woman! Ashtar here. We are now putting the final touches on the arrangements that will finally bring us to your screens. The fallen are gently walking away one by one, giving us greater access to those we must reach. Dear one, it will be soon. Blessings to you.

Thank you Ashtar

Greetings White Buffalo Calf Woman! Ashtar here, once again. Shortly after coming across your screen, we will commence with your vision for landing. This will be your "coming out" party also, to the rest of the world. Blessings to you, dear one!

Thank you Ashtar

Saturday, April 24, 2010

Greetings White Buffalo Calf Woman! Ashtar here. Please learn to discern all that you see and hear. You have heard the term "all is not as it seems". We are moving forward with coming into your realm and should see you shortly. Stay within your light for protection. Blessings to you, dear one.

Thank you Ashtar

Tuesday, May 4, 2010

Greetings White Buffalo Calf Woman! Ashtar here. We are making huge progress, just as all our earth allies on beloved Mother Earth. It seems each day she struggles along, holding on to her very existence. Thanks to our beloved lightworkers, she has been getting all the love and help to make her progress to a new world. Dear one, stay in the "now" moment and help all those who need it; for once we come forward, many will be in the "fear" mode. Blessings to you, dear one.

Thank you Ashtar

Thursday, May 6, 2010

Greetings White Buffalo Calf Woman! Ashtar here. You see the beginning of destruction all around you, on your screens. Let it be known that everything is still on course for first contact and the beginning of a new world. Keep the faith, keep in the moment and keep drinking the water! Blessings to you, dear one.

Thank you Ashtar

Thursday, May 20, 2010

Greetings White Buffalo Calf Woman! Ashtar here. I am most happy to see both you and Daniel getting back into meditation. It is very needed at this time as the Council of Twelve has stated. Your focus, of course, is always Mother Earth and all of humanity, the animals, waters, plant and mineral life. The Council of Twelve has asked you to pray for the children to awaken. Our beloved Indigo's must soon take charge as this is their time. Once again, keep meditating, as this is very important at this time. Blessings to you, dear one.

Thank you Ashtar

Monday, May 31, 2010

Greetings White Buffalo Calf Woman! Ashtar here. We are slowly making movement forward in a timely fashion. We still plan to break through this year. It is of monumental concern to get into shape, both of you. We are pleased to see a positive movement has been taken in this direction. If ever you have any personal questions you would like answered, just ask; we are always at your disposal. Thank you for getting up so early for this communiqué. Blessings to you, dear one.

Thank you Ashtar

Monday, May 31, 2010 (con't)

Greetings White Buffalo Calf Woman! Ashtar here with many greetings from your friends and colleagues. There are many steps leading to announcements which are slowly making their way to each and every soul upon our dear Mother Earth. The oil spill in the gulf has everyone on edge at this time and rightly so. We are one step closer; the dark minions cannot keep this up and the furor amongst the people escalates. Dear one, keep praying and ask everyone else to do so too. The peoples voices are being heard. Thank you. Blessings to you, dear one.

Thank you Ashtar

Tuesday, June 8, 2010

Greetings White Buffalo Calf Woman! Ashtar here with plenty to talk about! First and foremost, also as I have stated to Daniel, I am glad to see the exercising routine taking place; the extra weight will come off very easily. Today, I also wish to express my extreme happiness over the loving energies you have put forth to family, friends and those you hardly know but are struggling just the same. You love the world and everyone who resides there but are understanding the need for loving detachment. It is necessary to keep your own level of vibration activated. This will become easier because it is something you have done many times previously but have just forgotten about. Thank you for engaging your helpers; they are more than willing to step up to the plate and help in any and all ways they can. Last but not least, we move ever forward in our journey to the people. The light is growing stronger and we know we are welcome. We just wait now for the go ahead from the Creator God. Dear one, thank you for taking down this message so early in the morning. Blessings to you.

Thank you Ashtar

Sunday, June 27, 2010

Greetings White Buffalo Calf Woman! Ashtar here. As you can see, things are coming forward in your life, that have to be dealt with. As you know, moving towards a 5D world, the 3D has to be left behind. It is o.k. to help others, but do not be dragged down into 3D energies. It is of the utmost importance, at this time, to keep your focus on the future 5D world. What is it you would like to see? Try to remember; you have "been there, done that" before, so to speak. It is confusing at times, yes, but does not need to be. Dear one, I welcome speaking to you at any time; just ask for assistance. Blessings to you, dear one.

Thank you Ashtar

Friday, July 9, 2010

Greetings White Buffalo Calf Woman! Ashtar here. As we move ahead with our mission, we are disabling those who do not function within the light. Everyday is important now; that we keep vigilant about spreading the light and sending it to Mother Earth as you have been doing quite faithfully lately. Thank you and keep pushing on in your own mission, even though everyday living becomes tough. Rise above it and it will go away as long as you just stay within your light and love. It really is so simple! We have talked of your fear and that too will simply fall away. You have been asking for healing and receiving. March on, my little warrior. We are nearing the end of our fight for the right to light! Blessings to you, dear one.

Thank you Ashtar

Thursday, July 15, 2010

Greetings White Buffalo Calf Woman! Ashtar here with greetings from family and friends. I must commend you for reading about the Emissaries. You can now understand the message in there for you. Yes, it will be a good book for Daniel to read also. This is how we sometimes gain knowledge. As you can see, the Emissaries have been helping Earth for a long time. Without their help, can you imagine for one moment, what the conditions on Earth would be like in 2010? I shiver to think of it. The Emissaries are no longer needed on Earth, have not been for some time, as our "Light Brigade", our beloved light workers, have taken over the helm. And what a job they are doing! This includes both you and Daniel. Keep spreading your light; it works more than you can possibly know. Blessings to you, dear one.

Thank you Ashtar

Monday, July 26, 2010

Greetings White Buffalo Calf Woman! Ashtar here with greetings from many. We wish to assure you everything is being done to bring forward that which you have been awaiting. We are working diligently behind the scenes to make this so. Dear one, keep meditating for it is the only one true connection we keep with you. The council knows you getting rid of some pent up energy yesterday; all is good. We had quite the laugh; you still have the spark! Blessings to you, dear one.

Thank you Ashtar

Thursday, August 5, 2010

Greetings White Buffalo Calf Woman! Ashtar here. Many are listening to Mr. H. on your radio program tonight. His mission, at this time, is to push forward with disclosure. He is one of the "Canadian Earth Allies" and will be one of the few to be successful in this matter. I would very much like you to listen to him tonight. More news to come. Blessings to you, dear one.

Thank you Ashtar

Wednesday, August 11, 2010

Greetings White Buffalo Calf Woman! Ashtar here with the greatest of news! The scales of justice have very well tipped over to our side. It will not be much longer now to disclosure. Dear ones, yes, I'm speaking to you also Daniel, let the party begin! Many thanks to all you have done in such a short amount of time. It has been a wonderful ride, has it not? Blessings to you both, dear ones.

Thank you Ashtar

Monday, August 23, 2010

Greetings White Buffalo Calf Woman! Ashtar here with greetings from family and friends. It looks like miracles will come true. The time is right for our mission on earth to start. We are wrapping up with the elimination of the Illuminati. Hold your hats, dear one! Blessings to you.

Thank you Ashtar

Monday, August 30, 2010

Greetings White Buffalo Calf Woman! Ashtar here with many greetings of love from friends and family. The time is drawing closer and it is good to see you taking some time out; taking some loving care for the self. You have given much to others but have rarely taken time for you. Please do more of this. It is now time for "you", dear one! Blessings to you, dear one.

Thank you Ashtar

Tuesday, August 31, 2010

Greetings White Buffalo Calf Woman! Ashtar here. No need for pills. Everything hurts; it is the grand transition taking place. It is not easy for the human body to go through this. Dear one, hang in there! Blessings to you, dear one.

Thank you Ashtar

Monday, September 20, 2010

Greetings White Buffalo Calf Woman! Ashtar here. It is time for us to be back on daily communication again. It is time for a huge shift on the planet and when this happens, you will be needed. As I have stated, oh so long ago, people will start arriving in your life who will be working along side you. Please keep meditating every day. It has been so good to see you back here on the ship for short visits. Dear one, it is time to move forward, in great leaps, with our plans. Blessings to you, dear one.

Thank you Ashtar

Tuesday, September 21, 2010

Greetings White Buffalo Calf Woman! Ashtar here once again. As you have just read, we have a plan in place that we think will be most beneficial to "all". Dear one, I have said these same words to you many times and wanted to give you some other words from the Federation, so you would know what I give you to be the truth. Blessings to you, dear one.

Thank you Ashtar

Wednesday, September 22, 2010

Greetings White Buffalo Calf Woman! Ashtar here. We will get right down to speaking of the energies of the last evening. Dear one, I know it is very difficult but you must try to stay calm. There is so much going on around you that you cannot sense or see at this time. Our dear Nick is only looking out for you, in his special way, for animals sense and see everything. Just try to give him as much comfort as you can, for in the long run, he loves you as much as you love him. The energies will be intense from now till what we call the 10-10-10, when a massive convergence of energy will be beamed all around Mother Earth. We do hope for many more souls to awaken or at least to understand that something "different" is happening and to start asking questions. Because of our love for humanity, we hope as many as possible will awaken to ascension. That is our mission; it is what we are here for. Blessings to you, dear one.

Thank you Ashtar

Thursday, September 23, 2010

Greetings White Buffalo Calf Woman! Ashtar here with greetings from many, many who love you. At this time, we are preparing a plan for fly-over's this year; I can tell you that much. We are not one's for naming dates. There will be no contact with earth at this time as there are many who need to awaken. It is the way to do this peacefully. In our hearts, we hope that many more will realize we mean no harm to anyone, nor to Mother Earth. We are here for ascension purposes only and have no ulterior motive. As stated before, there will be no contact but hope that the presence of some of our ships will give our dear light workers the fuel to move forward. Although we are not seen, we are always around and feel so much love from many on your planet. Dear one, blessings to you.

Thank you Ashtar

Friday, September 24, 2010

Greetings White Buffalo Calf Woman! Ashtar here. The various councils and I, have been in constant meetings regarding a "showing" upon your skies. We have come to some agreements on various topics but are still "ironing out", if you will, certain others. We know it is very frustrating for those upon the earth plane regarding "not much happening" from their viewpoint. We do wish something would have transpired long before now but that is out of our hands without permission from our "higher source".

You see, dear one, sometimes it can be frustrating all the way round! Blessings to you.

Thank you Ashtar

Saturday, September 25, 2010

Greetings White Buffalo Calf Woman! Ashtar here with greetings from family and friends. Thank you for meeting with us yesterday. Your input into our quandary was greatly appreciated. We are most assuredly prepared to make a final decision shortly. Once again, dear one, thank you for your help. Blessings to you.

Thank you Ashtar

Sunday, September 26, 2010

Greetings White Buffalo Calf Woman! Ashtar here with greetings from your fan club! Meetings and negotiations with the various councils are on-going but we are making tremendous headway. As you know, we are taking our time as we want to get this right the first time, with as little fear and pandemonium as possible. As each of your days pass, soon I hope to have some positive news for you to share with whomever you wish. Blessings to you, dear one.

Thank you Ashtar

Monday, September 27, 2010

Greetings White Buffalo Calf Woman! Ashtar here with greetings from many fans. Not much to relay to you at this time. Still, the time seems right for a viewing, at the very least. We still gather together for High Council meetings and gauge the reaction of a fly-by next month, if not, this year. Blessings to you, dear one.

Thank you Ashtar

Tuesday, September 28, 2010

Greetings White Buffalo Calf Woman! Ashtar here with many loving greetings. As we have stated, things are moving along. We hope that what is to transpire this week or next, will manifest, as this is part of the "old" moving along, "exit stage left", to make room for the new "enter stage right"! Keep calm, keep centered as all transpires, as the worst of it will be short lived. This will make room for all kinds of "miraculous" events to occur. It will all happen in quick succession. Blessings to you, dear one.

Thank you Ashtar

Wednesday, September 29, 2010

Greetings White Buffalo Calf Woman! Ashtar here with the usual greetings from loved ones. As you have read this morning, we have decided to move forth with that which we have discussed earlier on. We wish to show ourselves first; secondly, we will speak, then proceed with what is known as "First Contact". We know many will still be in fear, but we hope by moving forth in this manner, that we will have quite a few more awaken to our mission of peace and not that of annihilation that your main stream media is feeding the masses. There is a saying upon your earth; "Slow and steady wins the race." This is our goal; this is our mission! Blessings to you, dear one.

Thank you Ashtar

Thursday, September 30, 2010

Greetings White Buffalo Calf Woman! Ashtar here with the usual loving greetings from friends and family. We move ever closer, dear one, to the huge party we have so waited for! All will soon know of our existence, not just the few who dare to "dream big"! We commend all who have helped us get to this point in time and encourage each of you to give yourselves a pat on the back. We surely will, when we meet on the earth plane. Blessings to you, dear one.

Thank you Ashtar

Friday, October 1, 2010

Greetings White Buffalo Calf Woman! Ashtar here. Once again, another of your weeks have come to pass. Is it not that time almost does not exist anymore? These changing times, as I have stated previously, will all meld together to become as one instant in the annals of "time"! Dear one, keep moving forward, shine your light for ALL to see. WE ARE HERE! Blessings to you, dear one.

Thank you Ashtar

Sunday, October 3, 2010

Greetings White Buffalo Calf Woman! Ashtar here with greetings from oh so many! We push onwards on our journey and wish to say "Expect miracles shortly"! We have all been watching you and Daniel "let go" of a lot of things that were not needed any longer. You will feel better of this shortly, as I know of the attachment "humans" become to material goods. They once brought joy and beauty but it is now time to move on; make way for something else, something better to materialize. Thank you for this endeavor. Blessings to you, dear one.

Thank you Ashtar

Tuesday, October 5, 2010

Greetings White Buffalo Calf Woman! Ashtar here with the usual greetings from friends and family who love you. The "energy drive" that is called the "10-10-10" on Mother Earth's atmosphere, is fast approaching. Lie low for a few days as it will be very intense. Daniel will heal quite fast; as he says, he's not like others! Blessings to you, dear ones.

Thank you Ashtar

Wednesday October 6, 2010

Greetings White Buffalo Calf Woman! Ashtar here. Everything is heard and duly noted. No worries at all and I see that you are not. Miracles abound the closer your 3D world gets to 5D. Oh, the rapture! Everyone will be in such joy; the world will sing! It is very close, dear one. Start celebrating! As I have stated yesterday of your time, Daniel is doing well with little to no pain. An experience; nothing more, nothing less. Blessings to you, dear one.

Thank you Ashtar

Friday, October 8, 2010

Greetings White Buffalo Calf Woman! Ashtar here. Dear one, there are no worries. Please keep your eyes and your mind on the final days of joy. Nick has been trying to teach you both something; he does not like your mothers energy. Yes, he is excited when he sees her; what dog wouldn't when they know they are going to get a cookie. You have also noticed when the cookies are gone, so is Nick. He does not stay around for affection but immediately leaves the area. Dear one, it has been said time and again, to watch the animals and learn from them. Stay focused and stay strong. Blessings to you, dear one.

Thank you Ashtar

Saturday, October 9, 2010

Greetings White Buffalo Calf Woman! Ashtar here. Enjoy yourselves this next while. No worries, just joy! Everything will soon fall into place.

We are ever so near. Keep your eyes on the skies for a phenomenal sight. Blessings to you, dear one.

Thank you Ashtar

Sunday, October 10, 2010

Greetings White Buffalo Calf Woman! Ashtar here with loving greetings from many. Is it not beautiful to bathe in the pure light and love given freely to everyone today? We smile; it is as if many souls are bathing in something they know not of, but are enjoying it none the less. We wish to make a visual contact very soon, with the same energy permeating the earth when we are here. We disappear, it disappears. We reappear, it reappears. Till those who do not understand, do; this is how we wish to operate. For this to be a grand success, all souls must understand we come in peace and wish no harm. Dear one, enjoy the energy. Blessings to you.

Thank you Ashtar

Monday, October 11, 2010

Greetings White Buffalo Calf Woman! Ashtar here with loving greetings. We feel for so many of our group who must go through daily hardships. We can only say, the end of that is very, very near. It has been a long road for many but with hidden benefits. We shall come at the right moment to benefit our cause. This is how it must be. The wait is literally at an end and we stand with baited breath. Blessings to you, dear one.

Thank you Ashtar

Tuesday, October 12, 2010

Greetings White Buffalo Calf Woman! Ashtar here with loving greetings from family and friends. The time is now; it cannot come soon enough, as they say! We await the final command to move forward. Rest up; the real work is just beginning! Blessings to you, dear one.

Thank you Ashtar

Wednesday, October 13, 2010

Greetings White Buffalo Calf Woman! Ashtar here with loving greetings from family and friends. The cheers that we hear around the world this day, are echoed from the higher dimensions. Is it not a wonderful feeling when the whole world is united in joyous celebration? We wish for this to be an everyday feeling; one of a loving nature, a coming together all over the world. Everyone sets aside their differences and becomes one with the whole. This day is here. Blessings to you, dear one.

Thank you Ashtar

Thursday, October 14, 2010

Greetings White Buffalo Calf Woman! Ashtar here with many loving greetings. We are so close to starting the mission; we await our final go ahead, moment by moment of earth time. The world in general, is on such a high state of gratitude at the moment. We sing praises ourselves. This is how it should be everyday; how it eventually will be. Stay in gratitude and joy, dear one! Blessings to you.

Thank you Ashtar

Friday, October 15, 2010

Greetings White Buffalo Calf Woman! Ashtar here, always with loving greetings from many who love you. As with previous communiqués, we gather momentum and wait out for the final go ahead. We know it is difficult at times to remain patient, but all is well and will continue to be so. So carry on; the time is ever near. Blessings to you, dear one.

Thank you Ashtar

Saturday, October 16, 2010

Greetings white Buffalo Calf Woman! Ashtar here with loving greetings from many. We are forging ahead; awaiting the final "go". It is a "must" that we all hold steadfast to the dream that is about to begin for all upon earth; the dream of freedom, peace and fairness to all with no boundaries to hold one back. Blessings to you, dear one.

Thank you Ashtar

Sunday, October 17, 2010

Greetings White Buffalo Calf Woman! Ashtar here with many loving greetings. The tides are changing very quickly and events are standing ready to happen. You are being given a lot of free time to prepare yourself for those who will come. When seeing them for the first time, it will be an instant recognition. There are also those on the earth plane who you will also be working with, those you have kept in contact with, those very close. Prepare yourself, dear one. Blessings to you.

Thank you Ashtar

Monday, October 18, 2010

Greetings White Buffalo Calf Woman! Ashtar here with loving greetings from family and friends. One day, dear one, we will appear in the skies as if by magic. From there on, nothing will ever be the same again. It is to be understood by all, that everything must move forward into a new reality or fade away as if it never were. This will be difficult for many, so at this time, much compassion is needed. It is everyone's own choice whether to ascend or not. The only thing that can be done is to give the facts and "let the chips fall where they may". Rest up, dear one, for there is much work to be done. Blessings to you.

Thank you Ashtar

Tuesday, October 19, 2010

Greetings White Buffalo Calf Woman! Ashtar here with the usual many, many greetings. Shine brightly, dear one, for we are right there with you. The time is here for the great celebrations to begin. Rise up to the occasion, for it is time to be, do and think positive, loving thoughts. Blessings to you, dear one.

Thank you Ashtar

Wednesday, October 20, 2010

Greetings White Buffalo Calf Woman! Ashtar here with many greetings from those who are wanting to give out hugs once again. Hold on to those light-filled thoughts; we have our go ahead but are awaiting our perfect moments to show up in not just a few ships here and there, but quite a few ships at different spots all over Mother Earth. This will happen, dear one; fear not. Just fill your mind with light, love-filled thoughts. Blessings to you.

Thank you Ashtar

Thursday, October 21, 2010

Greetings White Buffalo Calf Woman! Ashtar here with many loving greetings. We are moving forward through this time of stillness, for this is what is taking place at this time. It is a period of quiet stillness before the very chaotic, hectic energy unfolds upon the planet. We ask everyone to move through their days with joy and a clear picture of peace, love and beauty for the future of the planet; also a knowingness that everything is fine and all is as should be. Blessings to you, dear one.

Thank you Ashtar

Saturday, October 23, 2010

Greetings White Buffalo Calf Woman! Ashtar here with loving greetings from those you wish to see again. Keep on the path, dear one; enlightenment for all will take place very soon. Do not fill your mind with the mundane everyday goings on, but with light, love-filled thoughts of the future. It is here! The time is now! Blessings to you, dear one.

Thank you Ashtar

Sunday, October 24, 2010

Greetings White Buffalo Calf Woman! Ashtar here with the usual loving greetings. Dear one, I know you will be so excited to see your family and friends once again. The day is drawing closer when you will be able to come and go as you please; always remembering that you have a very important mission on earth. Dear one, there will be literally thousands who will flock to see you, hear what you have to say and to just be in your presence. Enjoy your "downtime", dear one, while you still have it, for your life will shortly do a complete one eighty. Blessings to you.

Thank you Ashtar

Monday, October 25, 2010

Greetings White Buffalo Calf Woman! Ashtar here with greetings from many. The time is approaching when many of our earth allies will be very busy paving the way for the lightworkers to come forth and reveal themselves. I tell you the task will be very daunting at times and frustrating in the least. Let the dust settle where it may; not all will listen or be interested. We can only hope for the best. Blessings to you, dear one.

Thank you Ashtar

Tuesday, October 26, 2010

Greetings White Buffalo Calf Woman! Ashtar here with greetings from many. Very shortly, a window of opportunity will open for another major sighting. This will be greater than the last, over New York. Keep your eyes on the news the next few days for what will be seen by many. The scope of what we are undertaking is huge for us, and of course, for humanity. Blessings to you, dear one.

Thank you Ashtar

Wednesday, October 27, 2010

Greetings White Buffalo Calf Woman! Ashtar here with many loving greetings from family and friends. We monitor very closely, the changes in energy on and around Mother Earth. We see the light has grown so much this past year, that it is advisable to us to go ahead with our sightings. We are so pleased that we are at this point in time where we are able to do so. We advise our Command members on earth; "All hands on deck"! Blessings to you, dear one.

Thank you Ashtar

Thursday, October 28, 2010

Greetings White Buffalo Calf Woman! Ashtar here with loving greetings from many. Our mission, we hoped, was to start a few months ago, but the dark and their minions had refused to give up the fight. I am most proud to say that only a few are still trying to upset the apple cart. It is not working, as the consciousness around your planet has grown much more than the dark can presently handle. You know, dear one, what this means for us. The party begins! Blessings to you, dear one.

Thank you Ashtar

Saturday, October 30, 2010

Greetings White Buffalo Calf Woman! Ashtar here. I will keep this short due to lack of paper on your part. Do not, I repeat, do not give up on us. Our mission is a go ahead. I know you are not privy to what is happening here but we are on target. Blessings to you, dear one.

Thank you Ashtar

Sunday, October 31, 2010

Greetings White Buffalo Calf Woman! Ashtar here with loving greetings from beyond your realm. Mother Earth continues to adjust herself through earthquakes, volcanoes and typhoons. To put it in much simpler terms, she is adjusting herself to the new world; shaking off what she does not need to take. This, dear one, is what anyone on the ascension path needs to do; shake off what is not needed, hence, all the "symptoms" everyone is having. When it all gets to be overwhelming, this is when rest is needed. It is that simple. Tell Daniel not to be overwhelmed going back to work; his symptoms will be very little. He will be worked on, of course, when he returns home, where he can rest. Only two months remain in this your year 2010, so we will "bump up" the sightings. Blessings to you, dear one.

Thank you Ashtar

Monday, November 1, 2010

Greetings White Buffalo Calf Woman! Ashtar here with many greetings from loved ones. This day is the beginning of the second last month of this year. When we, the Galactic Federation, look back over this past year of your time, we see that much progress has been made. It is to the point now where the light is so strong, the dark cannot survive. There are a few, not many, who hang around thinking everything will go their way once again. This will not be so and we all look forward to a quick, few surprises coming your way. Blessings to you, dear one.

Thank you Ashtar

Tuesday, November 2, 2010

Greetings White Buffalo Calf Woman! It is I, Ashtar. It is imperative for everyone at this time, to live in the moment. Living in the moment may include thinking of what your world is like outside your doors. Is it a peaceful, loving world that you see? If it is, in the moment, it will BE THAT! Do you see? The way you perceive things is how they are. You are the creator of your own reality. And this is ascension. Blessings to you, dear one.

Thank you Ashtar

Wednesday, November 3, 2010

Greetings White Buffalo Calf Woman! Ashtar here with greetings from loved ones and friends. You are entering a time of powerful energies; take time for the self. Days turn to weeks, of your timeline and before you know it, you will be into the timeline of 2011. Take this time to become stronger, overcome your insecurities and be at one with Mother Earth and all her inhabitants. Blessings to you, dear one.

Thank you Ashtar

Thursday, November 4, 2010

Greetings White Buffalo Calf Woman! Ashtar here with many loving greetings from your "galactic fan club"! We see your days passing and the hopes for the planet and mankind. All is taken into consideration and plans are made. We then send out the appropriate energies for the cleansing, with hopes that many more will awaken and push forward. Whatever the mass consciousness thinks, for a certain period, for instance, one of your days, then this is what transpires for that time period. It is all a thought process in motion, so to speak. We hope, very shortly, to move forward with another major sighting, one that cannot be explained away. Blessings to you, dear one.

Thank you Ashtar

Friday, November 5, 2010

Greetings White Buffalo Calf Woman! Ashtar here with the usual loving greetings from many beyond your realm. This month is very important as far as energies are concerned and should be treated as such. Many will feel a shift this month and should continue into December. Blessings to you, dear one.

Thank you Ashtar

Sunday, November 7, 2010

Greetings White Buffalo Calf Woman! Ashtar here with greetings from many. You know who you are, dear one, and we know those of you on Earth are hungry to start your missions. This will start in earnest in the new year. There is a time point for every aspect of our mission on earth and it all enfolds as and when it should. Blessings to you, dear one.

Thank you Ashtar

Monday, November 8, 2010

Greetings White Buffalo Calf Woman! Ashtar here with loving greetings from many. At this time, dear one, it is important to stay on track, true to yourself. Only you know what is best for you in the end. Allow yourself the time to meditate for it is important. Blessings to you, dear one.

Thank you Ashtar

Tuesday, November 9, 2010

Greetings White Buffalo Calf Woman! Ashtar here with loving greetings from friends and family. Your journey back to consciousness is quite a ride with a lot of inner work to do. You, dear one, are coming along in leaps and bounds. Enjoy the day, everyday! This situation will soon change for the better. Blessings to you, dear one.

Thank you Ashtar

Wednesday, November 10, 2010

Greetings White Buffalo Calf Woman! Ashtar here with greetings from many. Rest up, as tomorrows energies will be very uplifting. Meditation is called for on this day; thoughts of a loving, peaceful new world. Blessings to you, dear one.

Thank you Ashtar

Thursday, November 11, 2010

Greetings White Buffalo Calf Woman! Ashtar here with loving greetings from many. Everyone is going through the same energies, one way or another, even though they may not realize the "what or whys". It is only fair, is it not, that everyone be given a fair chance? Did you yourself, not see a difference with these energies today; a little easier to integrate? That does not mean they were not potent; they were even more so than 10-10-10, but it is easier now for you to deal with them. It is not everyday a soul gets a chance to experience what is happening on the earth plane at this time. Enjoy the ride! Be joyous, with a smile on your face and laugh, laugh, laugh! Blessings to you, dear one.

Thank you Ashtar

Monday, November 15, 2010

Greetings White Buffalo Calf Woman! Ashtar here with loving greetings from many. Your days are getting shorter; another season soon making its way in. The energies will be intense; rest when you are able. Know that everyone is fine and are where they should be in this ascension period. Change is inevitable, so just go with things as they happen. Blessings to you, dear one.

Thank you Ashtar

Tuesday, November 16, 2010

Greetings White Buffalo Calf Woman! Ashtar here with loving greetings from many. We are always available to talk to whenever one should want. Many do not even know, at this time, of our existence. This will be the first important step; revealing ourselves. This is where the fear will come and this is where our ground crew will be needed; to calm the masses. Then everything else will fall into place with ease and grace. Blessings to you, dear one.

Thank you Ashtar

Wednesday, November 17, 2010

Greetings White Buffalo Calf Woman! Ashtar here with loving greetings from many. The consciousness of every individual has risen substantially;

no matter if they are following the path of ascension or not. It is quite obvious to those who are on the path, that this is what they have chosen and will succeed. Time moves ever forward more quickly and then the party begins! Blessings to you, dear one.

Thank you Ashtar

Thursday, November 18, 2010

Greetings White Buffalo Calf Woman! Ashtar here with greetings from many. Today was a day of rest, the energies have lessened. This will be the name of the game for awhile; high energies one day, rest period for awhile and so on. We know it is very uncomfortable but necessary. We, of the Federation, wish nothing but the best for those upon the earth plane. Blessings to you, dear one.

Thank you Ashtar

Saturday, November 20, 2010

Greetings White Buffalo Calf Woman! Ashtar here with loving greetings from many. You know who you are and what your task is; you just have to have more conversation with the higher self. Dialogue will make it all come back, dear one! It is a process, a journey not to be rushed through. Blessings to you, dear one.

Thank you Ashtar

Tuesday, November 23, 2010

Greetings White Buffalo Calf Woman! Ashtar here with loving greetings from many friends and family. We are reaching the critical point where matter reaches the far reaches of density. It will be but the blink of an eye and your world will be changed forever. Meditate on this daily, dear one! Blessings to you.

Thank you Ashtar

Wednesday, November 24, 2010

Greetings White Buffalo Calf Woman! Ashtar here with loving greetings from many. The time draws near when a mass awakening must happen. We have a mandate that must move forward and that time is very near. That is when the work begins; to calm the masses till they can make a conscious decision for themselves; to ascend or continue "as is" somewhere else. The choice is with the individual. Blessings to you, dear one.

Thank you Ashtar

Thursday, November 25, 2010

Greetings White Buffalo Calf Woman! Ashtar here with loving greetings from many. We will start this communiqué with a warning that I must give to all. It is imperative that all "LISTEN TO WHAT THE HEART SAYS". Not all souls are on the same level of consciousness, therefore not everyone's perception of what is to be will be the same. Listen to the heart, not the head; not the mind. The mind fills up with too many facts; too much thought. It is like a jigsaw puzzle with many, many pieces that a soul is desperately trying to fit together. It is not that hard. Do not make it so difficult. When you hear facts, does it make the heart sing? Do you feel excitement? Or does your energy level drop significantly all of a sudden? All souls have feelings. Just trust. Blessings to you, dear one.

Thank you Ashtar

Saturday, November 27, 2010

Greetings White Buffalo Calf Woman! Ashtar here with loving greetings from friends and family. Today has marked another milestone in our ongoing struggles with the dark cabal. We have made a desperate move forward and it has paid off significantly. You see in your news, movement from our earth allies to educate the masses of the deception they have been under for eons of time. Disclosure is happening now and will pick up great strides within the coming weeks. There is no turning back. Blessings to you, dear one.

Thank you Ashtar

Sunday, November 28, 2010

Greetings White Buffalo Calf Woman! Ashtar here with loving greetings from friends and family. Today is the massive leaks that will continue on for awhile, leading up to our public disclosure. Sit back, do your work and enjoy the ride. Blessings to you, dear one.

Thank you Ashtar

Monday, November 29, 2010

Greetings White Buffalo Calf Woman! Ashtar here with loving greetings from many. In order for the human form to become a fully conscious light being, some stress and discomfort will be felt. It is best, at this time, to rest and just go with it as much as possible. Drinking a lot of pure clean water is also a must. As I have previously stated, over the next few weeks, the official disclosure process will be underway. Clearly, evidence of this is being broadcast at this time. Stay in the moment and enjoy the ride, dear one. Blessings to you.

Thank you Ashtar

Tuesday, November 30, 2010

Greetings White Buffalo Calf Woman! Ashtar here with loving greetings from many. As we move into the next weeks of your timeline, more information will come out, each more intense than that before. We ask each and every one to sort through the info; take that which most interests the individual. Trying to keep up with all of it, I'm afraid, will be overload. For those of you who have been awaiting these announcements, it will indeed be a very merry time for all leading into 2011. Blessings to you, dear one.

Thank you Ashtar

Wednesday, December 1, 2010

Greetings White Buffalo Calf Woman! Ashtar here with loving greetings from friends and family. As we move forward, more and more light permeating the earth and opening up the hearts of many on earth. In the coming days, more and more facts will be appearing in the media. It is important to take and believe what is for you, not what others think you should believe. You know this and are doing a wonderful job of standing in your own truth. But remember, it is wise to tell others your beliefs, but, a master to let others decide for themselves. Blessings to you, dear one.

Thank you Ashtar

Thursday, December 2, 2010

Greetings White Buffalo Calf Woman! Ashtar here with loving greetings from friends and family. Today's news from NASA will prepare the masses for "life beyond their own planet". There are many who are under the impression that this is the only planet that can sustain life. You, dear one, and many others know, of course, that this statement is false. We have promised much on the media circuit over the next few weeks and will certainly deliver. Blessings to you, dear one.

Thank you Ashtar

Saturday, December 4, 2010

Greetings White Buffalo Calf Woman! Ashtar here with loving greetings from many. At this time it should be repeated that one should absolutely read everything with discernment. Use that "gut" feeling that everyone talks about. In the end, it is your best friend, for it will never let you down. There is so much disinformation out there that we do not want our lightworkers to be betrayed. Blessings to you, dear one.

Thank you Ashtar

Sunday, December 5, 2010

Greetings White Buffalo Calf Woman! Ashtar here with loving greetings from many. It is with pleasant surprise, we see the light on earth growing ever so brightly. It will not be long now before the next set of information comes over your media. The dark cabal tries to attack back but they know this is not working. They will eventually give up. Then, dear one, comes the biggest party ever in this universe! Blessings to you, dear one.

Thank you Ashtar

Monday, December 6, 2010

Greetings White Buffalo Calf Woman! Ashtar here with loving greetings from many. Many more documents will be leaked very soon. Dear one, enjoy the moment as each leads to full disclosure. Our time is now! Blessings to you, dear one.

Thank you Ashtar

Tuesday, December 7, 2010

Greetings White Buffalo Calf Woman! Ashtar here with loving greetings from many. The days ahead will get a little complicated for many but for those who know what is happening, this will be a time of joy, of celebration. As you see, events are lining up for full disclosure soon. Blessings to you, dear one.

Thank you Ashtar

Wednesday, December 8, 2010

Greetings White Buffalo Calf Woman! Ashtar here with loving greetings from many. Where it comes to the media, it is up to the individual how they perceive the truth. Is the whole truth being told or is there an underlying truth? This is where the individual discernment comes in. As I have stated before, much information will come forth in the next few weeks. Be careful what you listen to. Blessings to you, dear one.

Thank you Ashtar

Thursday, December 9, 2010

Greetings White Buffalo Calf Woman! Ashtar here with loving greetings from many. It is without exception that there will be many versions of the same event coming out over the next few weeks and months. Not everyone is on the same page; ones truth is not necessarily another's. This is where mass confusion comes into play and why, thereafter we must come forward with a full disclosure. This will be the "storm before the calm". Be ready, dear one! Blessings to you.

Thank you Ashtar

Friday, December 10, 2010

Greetings White Buffalo Calf Woman! Ashtar here with greetings from many. At this time, it is best to go within ones heart to look for answers to questions that are troubling you. What to do at Christmas, where to go, what to give, are all things that take up too much mind space. Relax and go with the flow, dear one. Blessings to you.

Thank you Ashtar

Monday, December 13, 2010

Greetings White Buffalo Calf Woman! Ashtar here with loving greeting from many. There will be more documents filtering out shortly; picking up steam as we go! This cannot be held back much longer as time is running out. 2011 will be a very busy year, when all of our earth allies will be busy with the masses. Blessings to you, dear one.

Thank you Ashtar

Tuesday, December 14, 2010

Greetings White Buffalo Calf Woman! Ashtar here with loving greetings from many. Today there was much celebration for the release of one of our major whistleblowers. And his work is just beginning! And you, dear one, will soon follow! Rest up; the time is near. Blessings to you, dear one.

Thank you Ashtar

Wednesday, December 15, 2010

Greetings White Buffalo Calf Woman! Ashtar here with loving greetings from many. There will be some very major important "leaks" coming out very shortly. Stay tuned; we are about to rock the world!" Blessings to you, dear one.

Thank you Ashtar

Saturday, December 18, 2010

Greetings White Buffalo Calf Woman! Ashtar here with loving greetings from many. We look from our lofty positions and see such goodwill at this time of year. Now, dear one, imagine living in that kind of environment all year long! This is what is to be in the higher dimensions, times ten! Very much something to look forward to. Blessings to you, dear one.

Thank you Ashtar

Sunday, December 19, 2010

Greetings White Buffalo Calf Woman! Ashtar here with loving greetings from many. It is told that at this time of year, one looks to the birth of the baby Jesus. We would like to elaborate on the "feeling" of joy one experiences through this celebration. JOY! LOVE! That is the all! When one experiences this and nothing but, then ascension is surely the goal. There is nowhere to go but up! Blessings to you, dear one.

Thank you Ashtar

Monday, December 20. 2010

Greetings White Buffalo Calf Woman! Ashtar here with loving greetings from many. All at once, dear one, will come a time when you will understand all; everything will just click into place. All the longing, all the heartache, all the joy, all the pain; it will all be understood. And then, dear one, you will fly! Blessings to you.

Thank you Ashtar

Tuesday, December 21, 2010

Greetings White Buffalo Calf Woman! Ashtar here with loving greetings from many. As the days roll by toward the end of one year and the start of another, many miracles will occur, if one just looks for them. Some things or circumstances that seem at a loss, will be free to come forward into your life if it is allowed. Look and find, dear one! Blessings to you.

Thank you Ashtar

Saturday, December 25, 2010

Greetings White Buffalo Calf Woman! Ashtar here with loving greetings from many. Dear one, this year of 2010 will soon come to a close, which will usher in the new, 2011. This year is going to see tremendous change; not only in our dear Mother Earth but in all who reside upon her. Many must make choices that seem beyond their perceptions. This is where our dear lightworkers come in; that much needed support system. As time passes, it seems life itself is at a standstill. This cannot be farther from the truth, as much goes on behind the scenes. Keep on with your vision of a new, peaceful world. Blessings to you, dear one.

Thank you Ashtar

Sunday, December 26, 2010

Greetings White Buffalo Calf Woman! Ashtar here with loving greetings from many. You, dear one, have had a major shift in consciousness; one that will take you to many places on Mother Earth. You are a teacher, therefore shall teach. Blessings to you, dear one.

Thank you Ashtar

Monday, December 27, 2010

Greetings White Buffalo Calf Woman! Ashtar here with loving greetings from many. Very shortly, we hope to get the ball rolling. 2011 is upon us and it is time for the great awakening of Mother Earth and all her inhabitants. There will be some upheaval but not for long. Then come the announcements! Blessings to you, dear one.

Thank you Ashtar

Tuesday, December 28, 2010

Greetings White Buffalo Calf Woman! Ashtar here with loving greetings from friends and family. We will start with what was read today in a channeling. We know it came off as sounding somewhat angry but that is not the case. It is so frustrating at times to see what is taking place that should not be. I think, dear one, we will leave it at that. Keep up with your meditation; it is very important. Blessings to you, dear one.

Thank you Ashtar

Wednesday, December 29, 2010

Greetings White Buffalo Calf Woman! Ashtar here with greetings from many. We are on the brink of disclosure; as you have heard, within the first few months of the new year. Sit tight; the waiting is almost over. Blessings to you, dear one.

Thank you Ashtar

Thursday, December 30, 2010

Greetings White Buffalo Calf Woman! Ashtar here with loving greetings from many. We have predisposed of many who refuse to give up the control of earth. The remaining few will try to create that which they can no longer. It is futile but they refuse to see it that way. A lot of changes are to take place in the new year and quite quickly. As the saying goes, "Things will never be the same again"! Blessings to you, dear one.

Thank you Ashtar

Friday, December 31, 2010

Greetings White Buffalo Calf Woman! Ashtar here with loving greetings from many. In the days to come, dear one, all will be laid bare for you to read. Do not despair, it may be just that you or others have changed course; all is not lost. This is something you know. This is why, we insist more meditation be done each and every day. Talk! We wish to speak also! Blessings to you, dear one.

Thank you Ashtar

YEAR
2011

Monday, January 3, 2011

Greetings White Buffalo Calf Woman! Ashtar here with loving greetings from many. As the days go by, so to will the heartache you experience, for as they say in your world "It's not over till the fat lady sings"! And, dear one, I'm not referring to you in that comment! As Daniel has just stated, if it is meant to be, it will come to you. No worries. Just remember, not every situation unfolds the way "our heads" deem it should unfold. BELIEVE IN YOUR MIRACLES, DEAR ONE! Talk your talk and walk your walk with head held very high. Very High! You are a beacon of light for all to follow. BE that light which you penetrate the world with. Be that energy! And then, do the miracles happen. Blessings to you, dear one.

Thank you Ashtar

Tuesday, January 4, 2011

Greetings White Buffalo Calf Woman! Ashtar here with loving greetings from many. We regard the news media on your earth as "silliness". The reporting does nothing but serve the ones who are leaving the world stage. Those of you who know better see through the illusion. This is the beginning of a series of what we like to term "wake-up" to the peoples who still sleep. Blessings to you, dear one.

Thank you Ashtar

Wednesday, January 5, 2011

Greetings White Buffalo Calf Woman! Ashtar here with greetings from many. It is in this day and age of technology, that it behooves me to say that much in the way of free technology has been kept from the peoples. This is to soon turn around and there will be no such thing as paying an electric bill again. This is just the beginning of many marvelous "firsts" that will excite everyone. Spread the word, dear one. Blessings to you.

Thank you Ashtar

Thursday, January 6, 2011

Greetings White Buffalo Calf Woman! Ashtar here with loving greetings from many. Your news media outlets are teeming with more and more news everyday that can be applied to the changes that are to take place. This, dear one, is only the tip of the iceberg, so to speak. The stories will get a little more "off the wall" as time goes by, making the masses step back and ask themselves some very hard questions. This is where our earth allies and lightworkers come forward with the answers. Blessings to you, dear one.

Thank you Ashtar

Friday, January 7, 2011

Greetings White Buffalo Calf Woman! Ashtar here with loving greetings from many. Rest up, dear one; stay focused on the end result. That is what is important now. In this, the year of 2011, every moment counts. Remember, dear one, it is all in the heart. ALL!! Blessings to you.

Thank you Ashtar

Sunday, January 9, 2011

Greetings White Buffalo Calf Woman! Ashtar here with loving greetings from many. You are feeling intense energies tonight, dear one; this will happen periodically. You are so use to living in the denseness, that to finally be introduced to the higher energies, takes some getting use to. Drink plenty of water tonight while this is happening and every other time you experience this feeling. Blessings to you, dear one.

Thank you Ashtar

Wednesday, January 12, 2011

Greetings White Buffalo Calf Woman! Ashtar here with loving greetings from many. The news on your media gives the impression of the world, in itself, in the utmost turmoil. Rise above this and know what it is about and that soon the Federation will be in contact and able to help. We will never allow the others to "win" at this childish game that is being played out. Blessings to you, dear one.

Thank you Ashtar

Friday, January 14, 2011

Greetings White Buffalo Calf Woman! Ashtar here with loving greetings from many. Today we have had some movement in our favor, towards disclosure. The time is ripening for our disclosure and landings. Keep your light burning brightly and keep your eyes to the skies! Blessings to you, dear one.

Thank you Ashtar

Sunday, January 16, 2011

Greetings White Buffalo Calf Woman! Ashtar here with loving greetings from many. Today's informal meeting was all about the "go-ahead". Expect the unexpected very shortly. All is well. Keep dreaming those wonderful dreams! The time is NOW! Blessings to you, dear one.

Thank you Ashtar

Tuesday, January 17, 2011

Greetings White Buffalo Calf Woman! Ashtar here with loving greetings from many. Today was a day of tying together some loose ends from previous meetings held. Our plan was always firm from what we could decipher happening upon earth at a certain time. Everything points at disclosure happening very soon. We are, at present, counting the days when we can all meet once again. Blessings to you, dear one.

Thank you Ashtar

Thursday, January 20, 2011

Greetings White Buffalo Calf Woman! Ashtar here with loving greetings from many. Each day passing is one step closer to disclosure and landings. Today, you witnessed more arrests being made of the "other side" on your media. This will continue until they are no longer around to disrupt that which they know cannot be stopped. You will also start to see some movement in the self through the activations you received last night. Let them happen; this is everything you know coming back to you. Just let it be. Blessings to you, dear one.

Thank you Ashtar

Friday, January 21, 2011

Greetings White Buffalo Calf Woman! Ashtar here with loving greetings from many. We slowly make progress towards our disclosure. Dear one, it is not far off! Let your aches and pains come and go. It is the body's way of getting rid of that which it no longer needs, thanks to the beautiful energies you received. Just let it all go! Keep smiling, dear one, for I see you doing more of that lately. Blessings to you.

Thank you Ashtar

Saturday, January 22, 2011

Greetings White Buffalo Calf Woman! Ashtar here with loving greetings from those who love you dearly. Dear one, it is not for us to give dates for what we know is going to eventually happen; but let me say this "It is so close, you can taste it"! Everything is commencing at a more rapid pace. True progression! Rest up and heal your body, dear one. The time is near. Blessings to you.

Thank you Ashtar

Sunday, January 23, 2011

Greetings White Buffalo Calf Woman! Ashtar here with loving greetings from home. It is good to see both you and Daniel keeping abreast of all that is going on with the big picture through the media. Remember though to use your discernment. Listen to your heart with everything you read and see. As you can see, there is a lot of forward momentum in this year, 2011. Dear one, start planning the party! Blessings to you.

Thank you Ashtar

Monday, January 24, 2011

Greetings White Buffalo Calf Woman! Ashtar here with loving greetings from many. Events are picking up in frequency; soon you will not be able to keep up with it all. At this time, we are starting to pressure the President to disclose our presence very soon. It won't be long now, dear one! Blessings to you.

Thank you Ashtar

Tuesday, January 25, 2011

Greetings White Buffalo Calf Woman! Ashtar here with loving greetings from many. As stated previously, always use discernment. Your heart will never lie to you. Today we have made much in the way of forward momentum. Keep positive; things are happening. Blessings to you, dear one.

Thank you Ashtar

Wednesday, January 26, 2011

Greetings White Buffalo Calf Woman! Ashtar here with loving greetings from many. We will, very shortly, be stepping up the sightings. Keep your eyes to the skies. The "games" are just about over and then it will be smooth sailing to disclosure. Blessings to you, dear one.

Thank you Ashtar

Thursday, January 27, 2011

Greetings White Buffalo Calf Woman! Ashtar here with loving greetings from many. Today we made some more progress; on our way! It really will not be long, dear one. There are those who are giving up their "positions of power", which bring us closer to being in touch with those we love dearly. Blessings to you, dear one.

Thank you Ashtar

Friday, January 28, 2011

Greetings White Buffalo Calf Woman! Ashtar here with loving greetings from many. As we move forward and there is much in the way of destruction around the world, think light, be light, do light and LOVE. This balances out the negativity or perceived negativity on your world, so we may move forward. Be excited, be in joy, and most of all, be in love for the grandest story of ALL TIME! Blessings to you, dear one.

Thank you Ashtar

Saturday, January 29, 2011

Greetings White Buffalo Calf Woman! Ashtar here with loving greetings from many. We make daily progress and will soon deem this mission to be a complete success. The party is nigh! Be clear with your visions and hopes for the future. Blessings to you, dear one.

Thank you Ashtar

Sunday, January 30, 2011

Greetings White Buffalo Calf Woman! Ashtar here with loving greetings from many. Today we push forward once again, clearing lower energies into the light. Dear one, take a deep breath, as all that must fall away will. Keep your chin up; you can do this. Blessings to you.

Thank you Ashtar

Wednesday, February 2, 2011

Greetings White Buffalo Calf Woman! Ashtar here with loving greetings from many. The massive changes are taking place in some areas of your world. Where there is much disruption, send light and love. Help us to help them. This will soon give way to a peaceful resolution for all, all over the world. This, dear one, is the beginning of the end of duality. Blessings to you.

Thank you Ashtar

Monday, February 7, 2011

Greetings White Buffalo Calf Woman! Ashtar here with loving greetings from many. We are ever closer to our destiny; please watch your news channel. Expect some very big changes soon. All is well. Blessings to you, dear one.

Thank you Ashtar

Wednesday, February 9, 2011

Greetings White Buffalo Calf Woman! Ashtar here with loving greetings from many. As you say in your world, "Things are heating up". It is time to set the world stage for a party that has never ever been seen before! My message tonight, dear one; "Get your party clothes ready"! Blessings to you.

Thank you Ashtar

Thursday, February 10, 2011

Greetings White Buffalo Calf Woman! Ashtar here with loving greetings from many. Today's "antics" will not be tolerated for long as the regime has come to the end of the road. Keep your eyes and thoughts on the peaceful resolution that is to come. Blessings to you, dear one.

Thank you Ashtar

Sunday, February 13, 2011

Greetings White Buffalo Calf Woman! Ashtar here with loving greetings from many. At an opportune time this next week, some significant info for you will come to you in a very surprising way. Enjoy! Blessings to you, dear one.

Thank you Ashtar

Wednesday, February 16, 2011

Greetings White Buffalo Calf Woman! Ashtar here with loving greetings from many. As the next few weeks progress, more of your questions will be answered as the veil slowly drifts away. Enjoy these last few remaining weeks as Nancy. Blessings to you, dear one.

Thank you Ashtar

Thursday, February 17, 2011

Greetings White Buffalo Calf Woman! Ashtar here with loving greetings from many. The energies increase and so do the aches and pains. The transformation, at times, is not easy; but persevere. It will truly be worth it in the end. Blessings to you, dear one.

Thank you Ashtar

Friday, February 18, 2011

Greetings White Buffalo Calf Woman! Ashtar here with loving greetings from many. We move forward and no skipping a beat! Time is winding down to "no time". What a celebration of all that was manifested in 3D! Congrats to all! Good work, team! Blessings to you, dear one.

Thank you Ashtar

Tuesday, March 8, 2011

Greetings White Buffalo Calf Woman! Ashtar here with loving greetings from many. We are counting down the days, yes, dear one, literally days till a huge announcement! Keep listening with your heart! You will know the exact timing. Blessings to you, dear one.

Thank you Ashtar

Wednesday, March 9, 2011

Greetings White Buffalo Calf Woman! Ashtar here with loving greetings from many. You will soon see the benefits of sitting with yourself over the past couple of years. Nothing is lost and much has been gained. Look forward! Blessings to you, dear one.

Thank you Ashtar

Friday, June 3, 2011

Greetings White Buffalo Calf Woman! Ashtar here with very exciting news. We have most of the dark cabal in house arrest and they are being processed for trial. It should not be long now, dear one. Keep looking to the skies for further evidence that disclosure is near. It is good to be in contact once again, dear one, for it is imperative we once again begin our talks. Blessings to you, dear one.

Thank you Ashtar

Wednesday, June 15, 2011

Greetings White Buffalo Calf Woman! Ashtar here with loving greetings from many. Your current timeline is winding down to proceed into a new 5D timeline that will be a benefit to the masses. Oh, the changes! We, of the Federation, are so proud of what was accomplished during this grand drama. A big thank you to all who have kept the vigil of a brand new earth, alive and well through the lower energy vibration. You have done well! We will have more communication leading up to the grandest party yet! Thank you and blessings to you, dear one.

Thank you Ashtar

Thursday, June 16, 2011

Greetings White Buffalo Calf Woman! Ashtar here with loving greetings from many. Today we will talk of the energies permeating earth at this time. They come in opposite increments; very strong for a few days, then lessen in their intensity for a few days. It is when they are at their most intense, when the human body seems to suffer; e.g.: getting rid of toxins and lower energy brings on headaches, sleepiness or as in yourself, cold-like symptoms with itchy eyes. Lay low for a day or two till you are feeling more like your old self. Look after number one! Blessings to you, dear one.

Thank you Ashtar

Wednesday, July 13, 2011

Greetings White Buffalo Calf Woman! Ashtar here with loving greetings from many. As in the past, the word "soon" has been used a little too often, unfortunately, as we thought "progress" was "progressing" faster than what eventually happened. Therefore, I will cease to use the word from here on in, dear one; instead I will say "the date is closing in". Dear one, make some time for your "I AM" presence during your day; this is most important at this time. Blessings to you, dear one.

Thank you Ashtar

Friday, August 26, 2011

Greetings White Buffalo Calf Woman! Ashtar here with loving greetings from many. We ask, on this day, to keep looking to your skies. There are those who wish to enter your apartment but are awaiting an "invite" from you. Maybe start a daily mantra; "Those light beings who are here to assist me at this time, I welcome you". It is time to start your mission, dear one, that mission that has been at the very centre of your heart for a very long time. As things get a little chaotic, stay in joy, in the moment, and no worries. Blessings to you, dear one.

Thank you Ashtar

Thursday, September 15, 2011

Greetings White Buffalo Calf Woman! Ashtar here with loving greetings from many. My, but how your time is flying! Dear one, there is an abundance of meetings taking place at this time; so many, in fact, the excitement here grows stronger every day. There are so many awaiting the reunions! Love is being sent to earth in staggering amounts. Mother Earth is lighting up like a precious jewel. Dear one, not long now; remember to please take time for the self. You are also deserving! Blessings to you, dear one.

Thank you Ashtar

We now find ourselves in the year 2012. The past five years of speaking with Ashtar and other members of the Galactic Federation, have been years of growing and self discovery for me. Up until 2006, I was not leading any kind of a spiritual life. During the early month's of 2006, I began to receive messages and visions from spirit. This continued throughout the rest of that year and in 2007 this progressed to the "transmissions" from the Galactic Federation. My life did a complete one eighty in a two year time span!

There are major changes that have taken place worldwide within these past few years and continue to do so now. We are currently going through a period of "ascension"; this is both a worldwide event and also a personal journey of each and every soul. It is not something to fear; to try to run and hide from. It is simply a dimensional change to a higher consciousness, a "graduation from high school to university"!!

We are all souls having a human experience, taking our own journeys, down our own paths of self discovery. From my heart, I wish each and every one of you the very best. May YOUR journey take YOU to the very place you call "home".

In love and light
Nancy Horn
White Buffalo Calf Woman
April, 2012